An Artist's Vision,
Twenty-Twenty

Author: Dan Wetta

Published by Daniel Wetta Publishing

Copyright 2015

Please visit Author Page:

http://www.amazon.com/Dan-Wetta/e/B00O6S0MNC

Table of Contents

Prologue

The first chapter of this second printed volume of my life's art work is about the birds. Many of us periodically dream that we can fly like a bird, so I wanted this book to begin with exploring the world of birds. Some of them, as shown in my art, are trapped in stain glass windows like the saints who are imprisoned in the windows of medieval cathedrals.

The second chapter pulls you into the whacky world of my cartoons. Most of these cartoons are "ruffs." Ruffs are preliminary sketches: unfinished cartoons that are submitted to cartoon editors in the hope that the idea will be liked. If the editors like the cartoon, they send it back to the artist so a finished version can be drawn. Personally, I think some of the theme and feeling of the original ruff is lost when you turn it into a finished drawing.

From there, I introduce you in the third chapter to some of my family, beginning with my late wife, Martha, pulling out her hair as she contemplates a mountain of paper work on her desk that she has to do before she retires in about a week. This is followed by a second cartoon showing a happy ending. Then I show several cartoons of my grandchildren and great grandchildren.

The fourth chapter, "Odds and Ends," is about this and that. In chapters Five through Seven, I relive some memories as far back as the 1930s.

The remaining chapters show art covering important issues of lions, tigers, boats, and why everybody wants to moo like a cow. There is a chapter that puts problems into perspective, one about motherly visions, and a couple of chapters exploring biblical and evolution themes. The book ends with my dream of an adventure in a run-of-the-mill town.

Chapter 1: Bird's Eye View

In my first printed, illustrated book, *An Artist's Life, New Orleans Framed,* I included a section on birds. They have always been a fascination for me in life, and it is no surprise that so much of my art tries to capture the feeling of what it is to be a bird and to be able to fly. Many people have told me that they have dreams where they are flying.

However, I wonder if there are still people whose philosophy is:

If God wanted people to fly, he would have given them wings.

I am starting off this new book with a special section honoring our feathered friends.

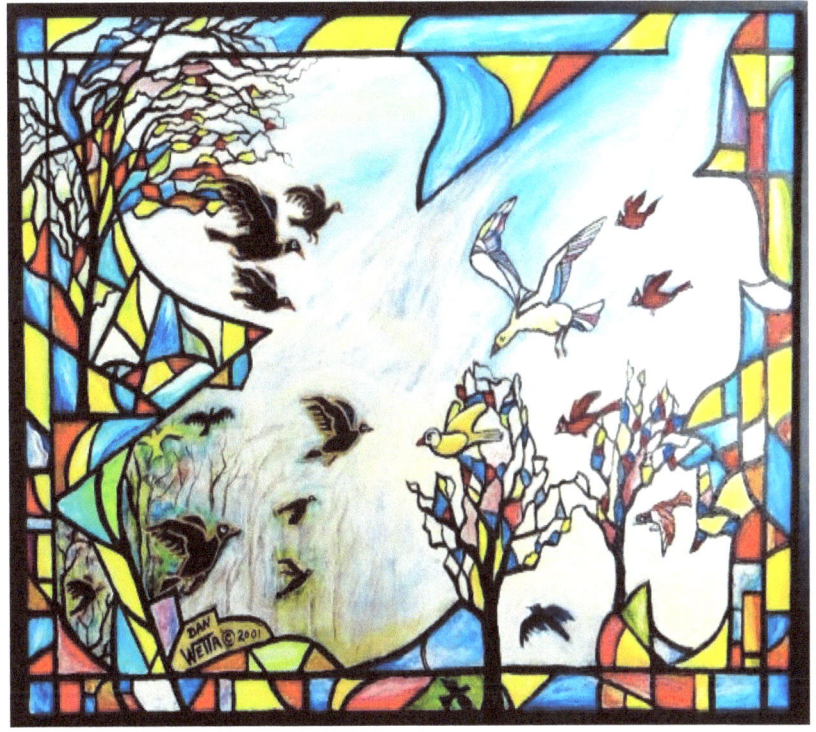

Title: Stained Glass Birds
Size: 24x36 inches
Medium: Acrylic on canvas
Copyright by Dan Wetta 2001

I took a beginner's course in stained glass media several years ago, but I just couldn't get the hang of cutting glass, so I decided to design stained glass scenes instead. "Stained Glass Birds" is one such example of my art that simulates stained glass.

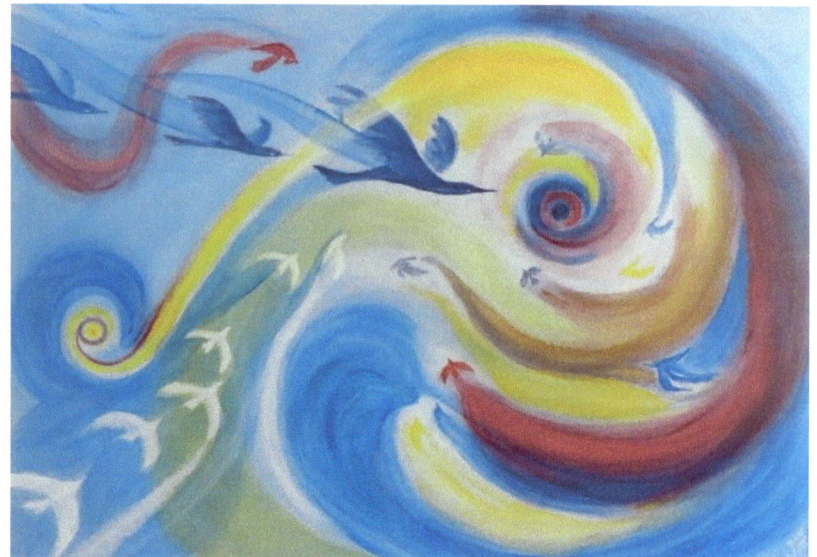

Title: Worm Hole in the Sky
Size: 24x20 inches
Medium: Acrylic on canvas
Copyright by Dan Wetta 1994

When I first heard of a worm hole in the sky, I wondered if the birds had heard about it. This painting has no scientific value. It represents a bird's eye view of the worm hole! The earliest birds are the ones who are closest to the hole, I suppose!

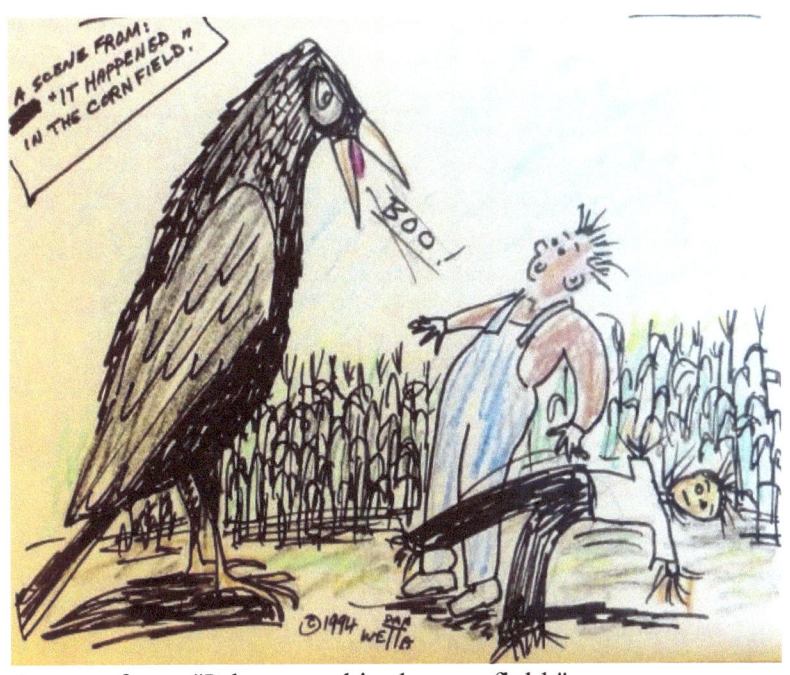

A scene from, "It happened in the cornfield."

Title: Boo!
Size: 9x12 inches
Medium: Mixed media on paper
Copyright by Dan Wetta 1994

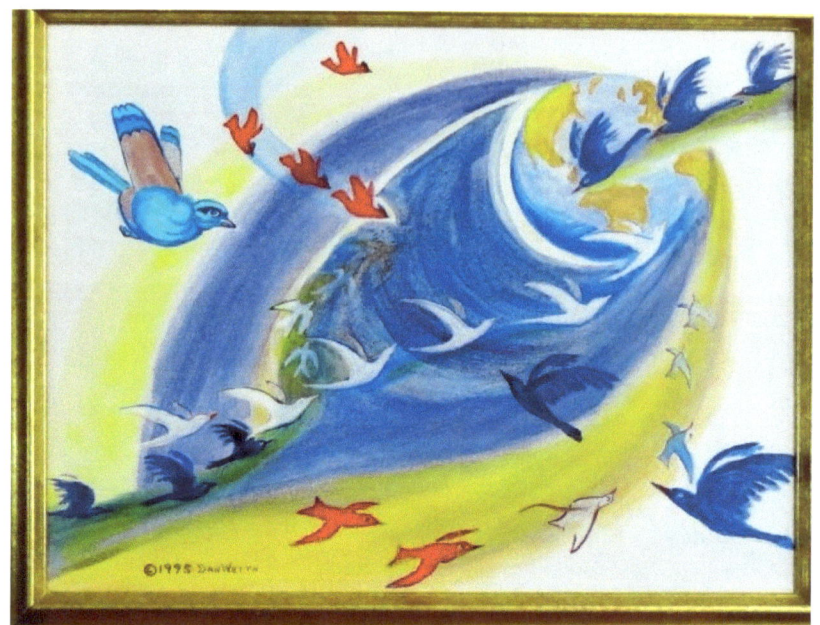

Title: Dizzy Birds
Size: 16x20 inches
Medium: Acrylic on canvas
Copyright by Dan Wetta 1995

    I got dizzy while painting these birds flying around in circles. At one time, I was painting so many bird pictures that I began dreaming that I could fly.

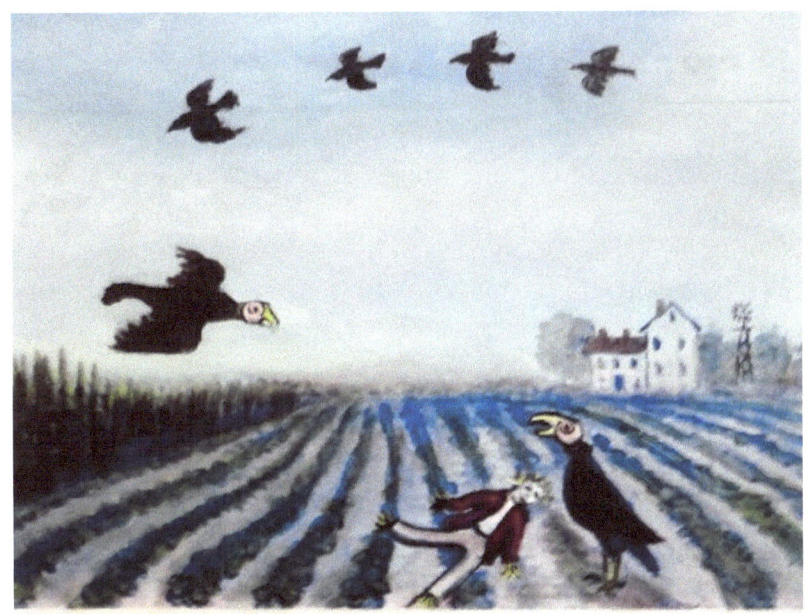

DON'T BOTHER - IT'S ONLY A SCARECROW

Title: Scarecrow
Size: 18x24 inches
Medium: Acrylic on canvas
Copyright by Dan Wetta 2003

Turkey buzzards have a sense of humor, too, you know!

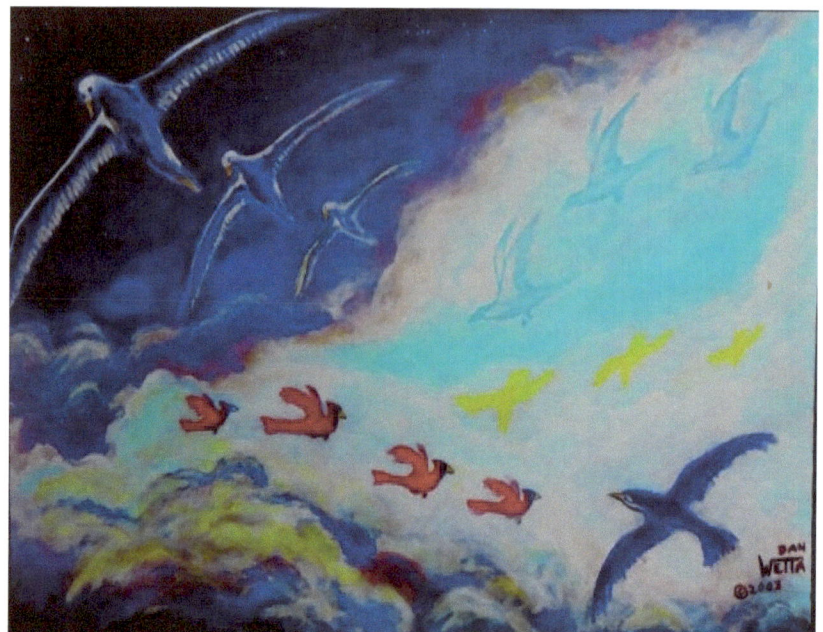

Title: Four Cardinal Scramble
Size: 30x30 inches
Medium: Acrylic on canvas
Copyright by Dan Wetta 2003

Birds flying in the earth's atmosphere remind me of fish swimming in water. The wings of birds move them through the air, same as the fins of fish propel them through the water.

On another note: Most people think angels have wings because artists paint them that way, but wings are useless once they get into space where there is no air.

The only people who have ever seen an angel are in the bible, and we can't ask them about this because the people who have seen angels are dead now.

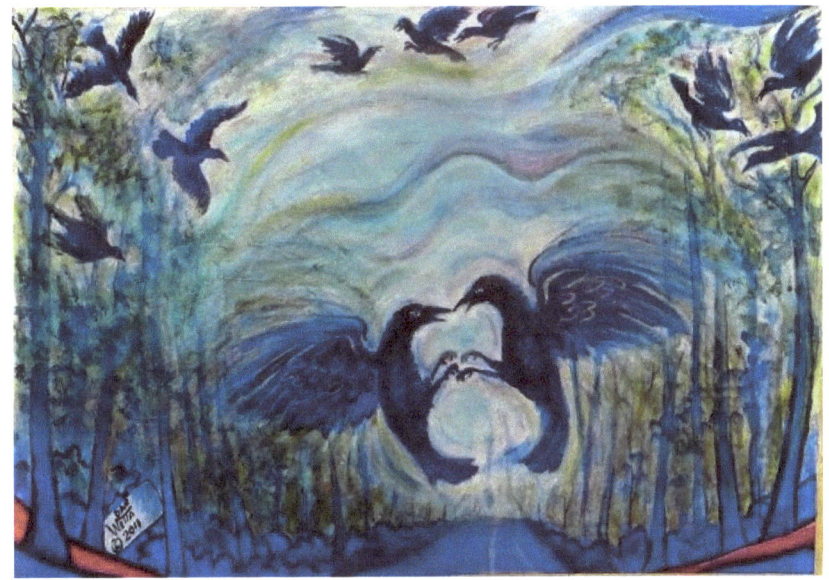

Title: Crows Fighting
Size: 20x30 inches
Medium: Acrylic on canvas
Copyright by Dan Wetta 2011

I was daydreaming as I walked along this two lane road lined with trees on both sides. Suddenly, I was startled to reality by a bunch of crows locked in battle. I didn't know whether to run or what, when two of them, fighting beak to beak, floated down right in front of my face!

I guess we scared each other, because when they saw me, they flew away.

I think that I was in the middle of a territorial dispute. Wings were flapping wildly, and feathers were floating all around me as the crows squawked insults at each other. But then all of a sudden, one flock of crows took off in defeat, while the winners flew to the tree tops and began a caw-caw song of victory.

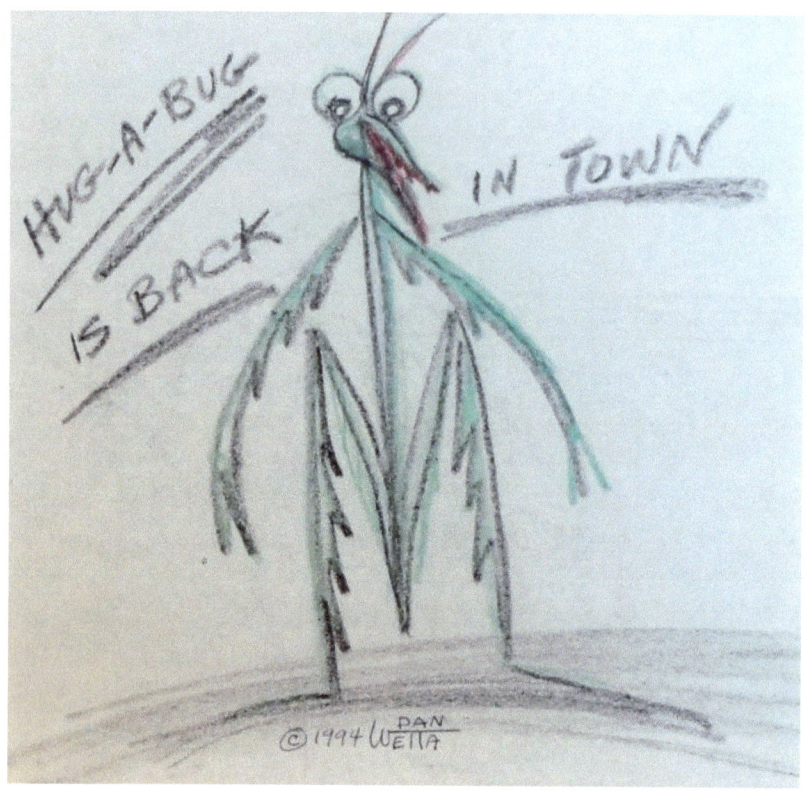

Title: Hug a Bug
Copyright by Dan Wetta 1994

I was walking in my neighborhood one day when a mocking bird landed right in front of me with a praying mantis in his mouth. I reacted instinctively and swung my walking cane at the mocking bird, and he dropped the mantis and flew away. The mantis seemed to be okay, and the mocking bird had disappeared.

Then I wondered if I had interfered with nature.

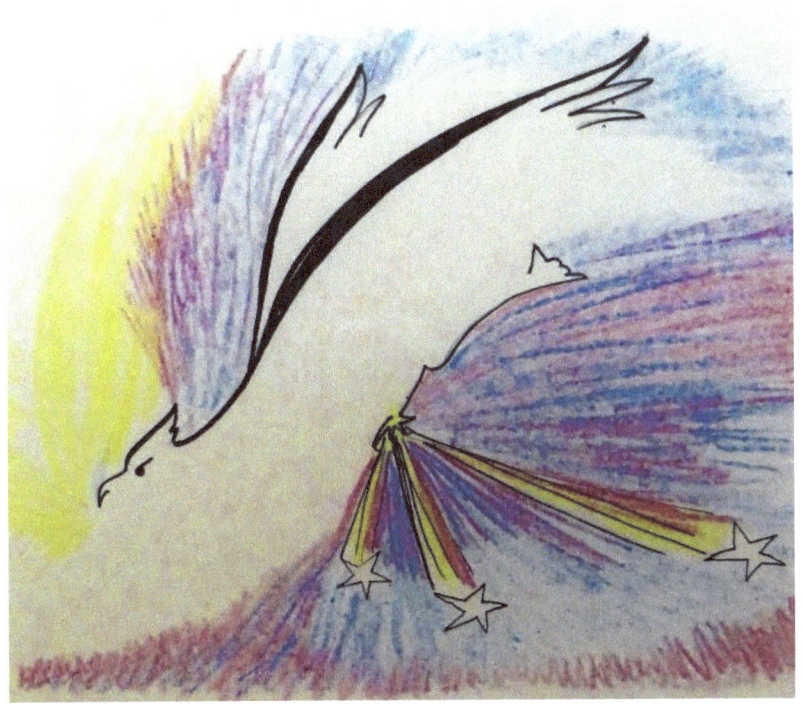

Title: Eagle Star
Copyright by Dan Wetta

If there is such a thing as a semi-abstract, that's what this one is.

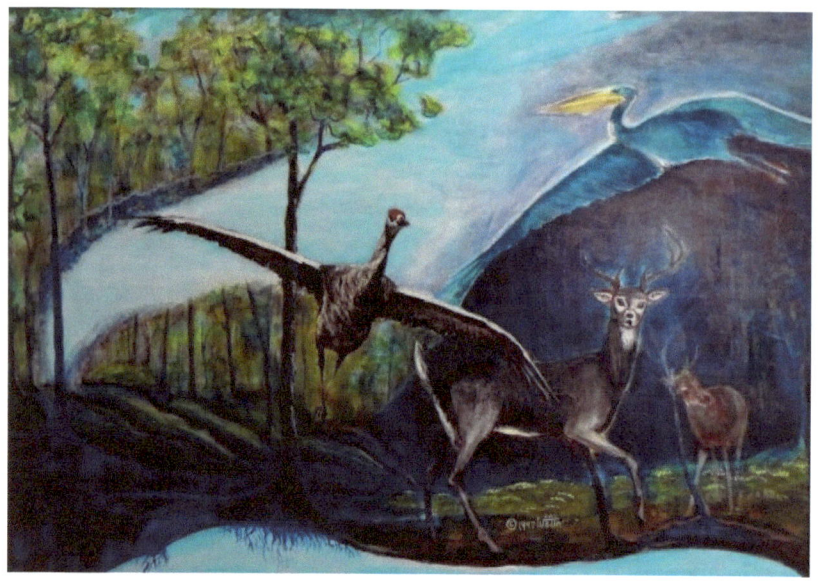

Title: Pelican, Goose, Deer
Size: 24x36 inches
Medium: Acrylic on canvas
Copyright by Dan Wetta 1997

The pelican and goose are confused because their sky has fallen into the woods. The close deer is puzzled by what happened. That deer in the background is unconcerned. He only wants to rub his antlers clean.

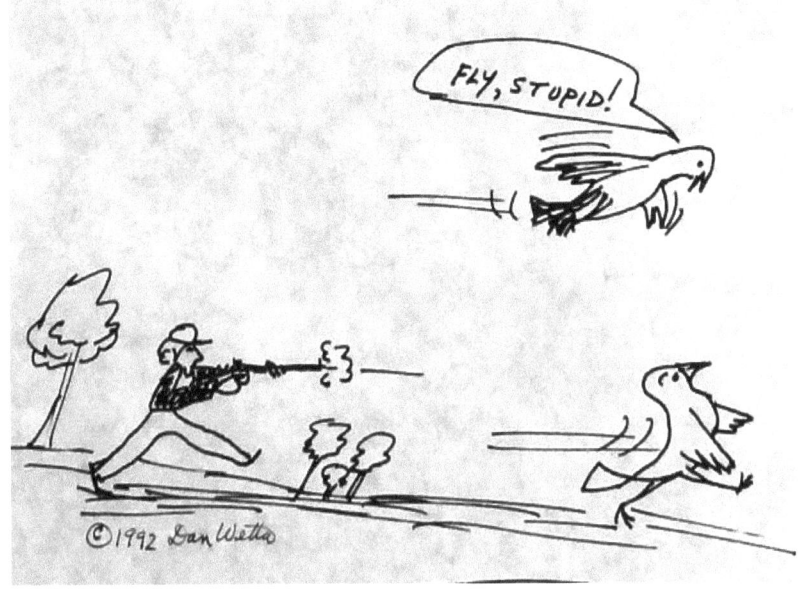

Title: Fly, Stupid
Copyright by Dan Wetta 1992

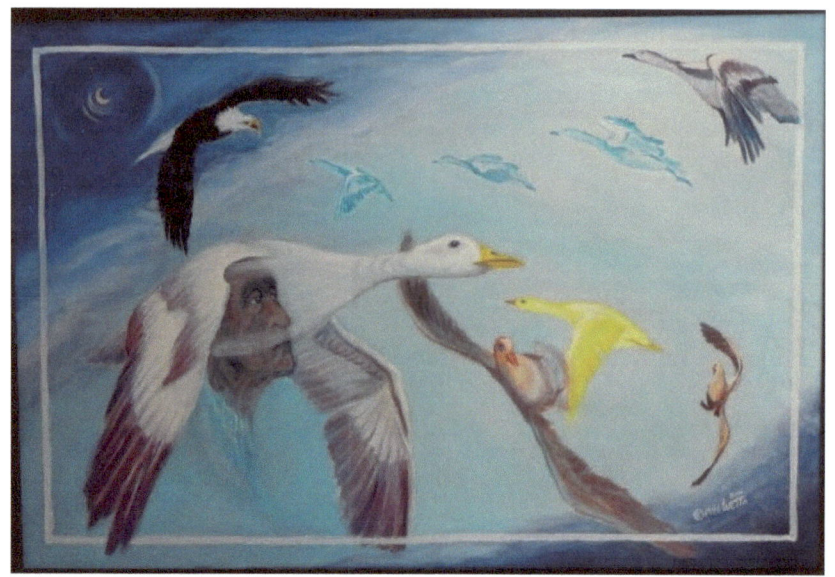

Title: Indian Vision
Size: 24x36 inches
Medium: Acrylic on canvas
Copyright by Dan Wetta 1996

Geese sometimes roll over on their backs in order to lose altitude.
Take a second look at the white goose.

I didn't start off with the idea of painting an Indian chief into this
scene, but those wing feathers reminded me of an Indian headdress, so
that is how the Indian chief got into my painting.

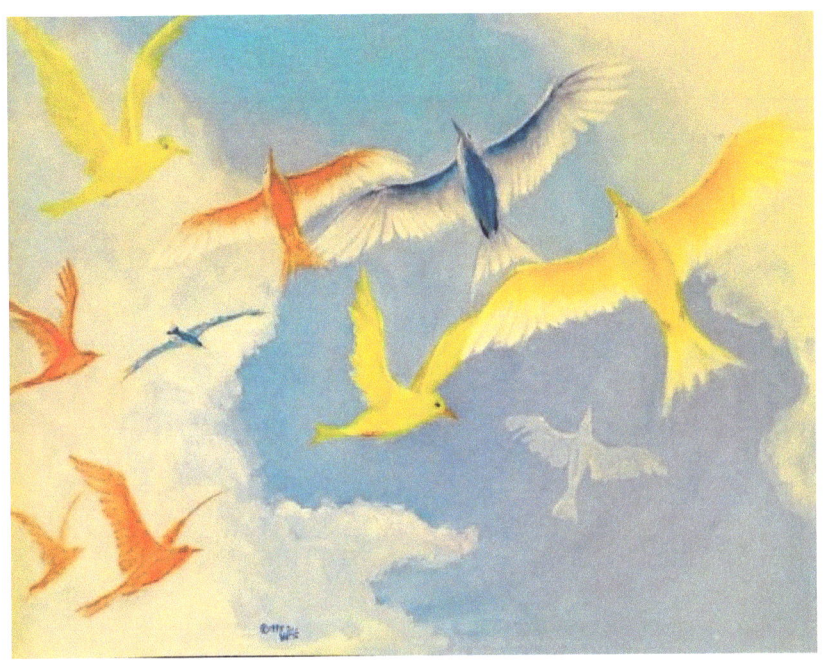

Red Yellow Blue Birds
Size: 24x36 inches
Medium: Acrylic on canvas
Copyright by Dan Wetta 1995

My son, Daniel, described this painting as a rendering of spiritual ascent, which surprised me. I thought that I was just experimenting with primary colors.

It just goes to show you that colors do have a strong influence on your feelings and emotions.

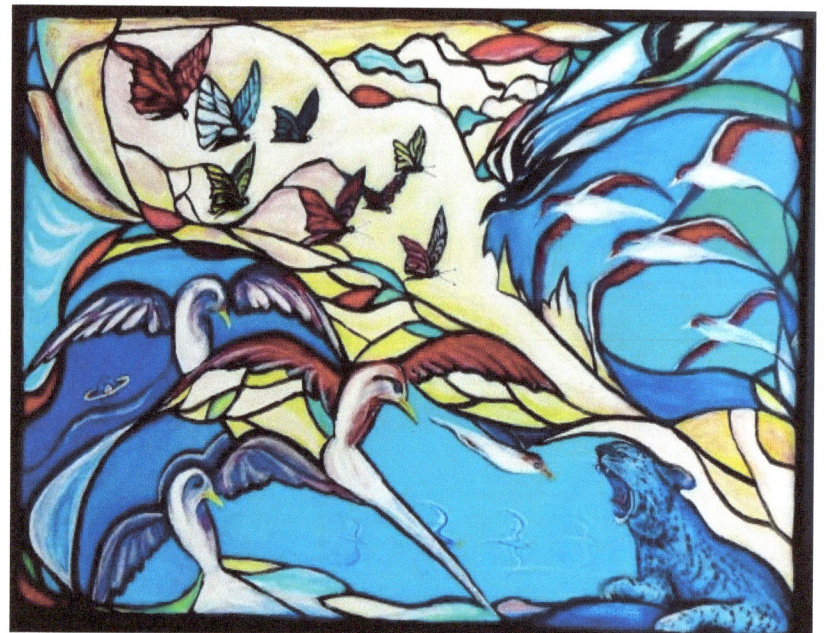

Title: Butterflies Birds and a Cat
Size: 24x36 inches
Medium: Acrylic on canvas
Copyright by Dan Wetta 1996

The birds are teasing the cat.

I should have put catbirds in the picture. Catbirds attack people too.

Once, when I was walking to K-Mart, I passed too close to a bush with a nest of baby catbirds, and a pair of catbirds began attacking me. They chased me for thirty yards or so and then flew back to their nest. I continued on to K-Mart.

On the way back, I walked on the other side of the street from their nest, but they recognized me and came after me again! I ran about one hundred yards to my condo before they gave up the chase.

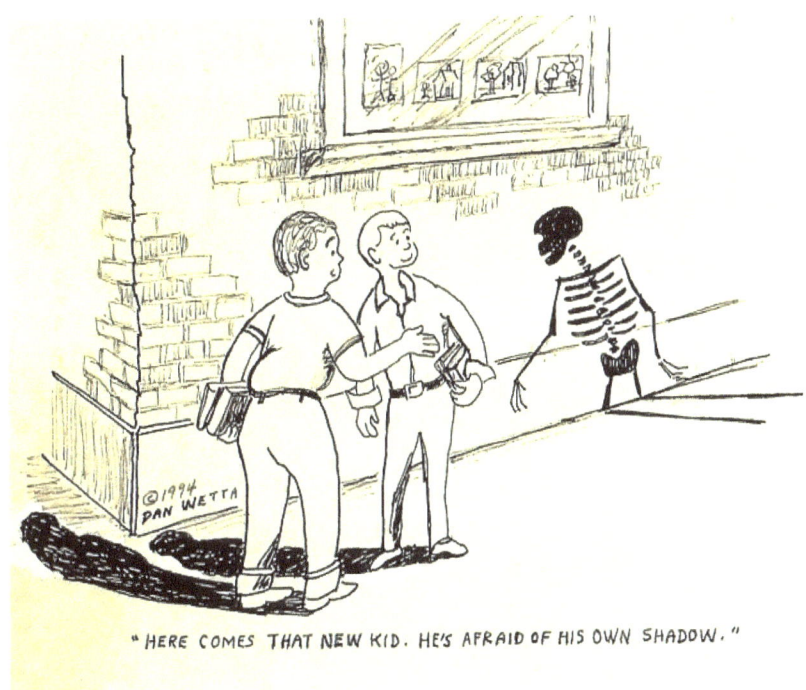

"HERE COMES THAT NEW KID. HE'S AFRAID OF HIS OWN SHADOW."

Title: Afraid of Shadow
Copyright by Dan Wetta

As soon as God created light, he created shadows.
Light and shadows did not evolve over a long period of time.

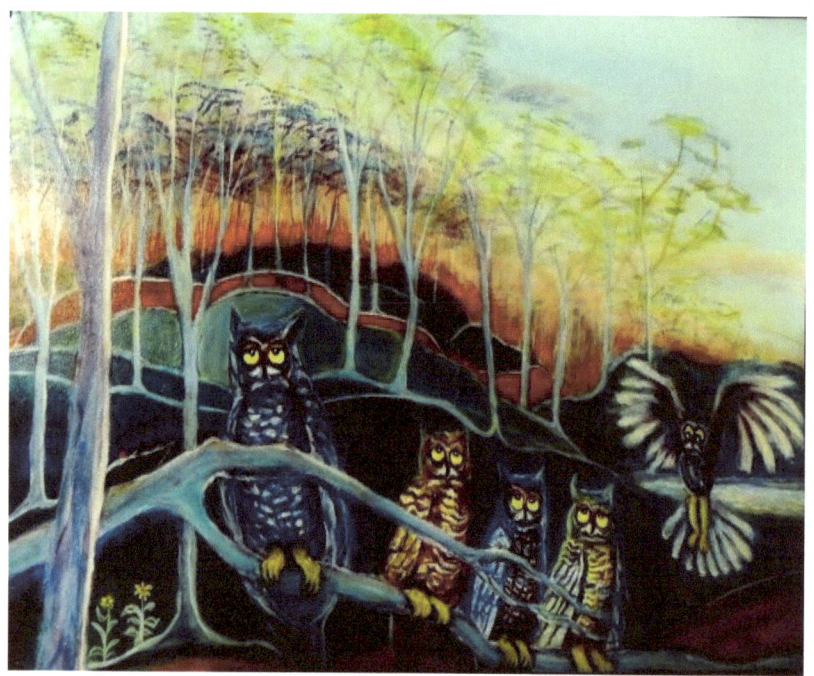

Title: Quiet, I'm Trying to Think!
Size: 20x30 inches
Medium: Acrylic on canvas
Copyright by Dan Wetta 1989

Daddy owl is trying to look wise.
Baby owl just wants to clown around and have fun.
What else is there to do in the woods?

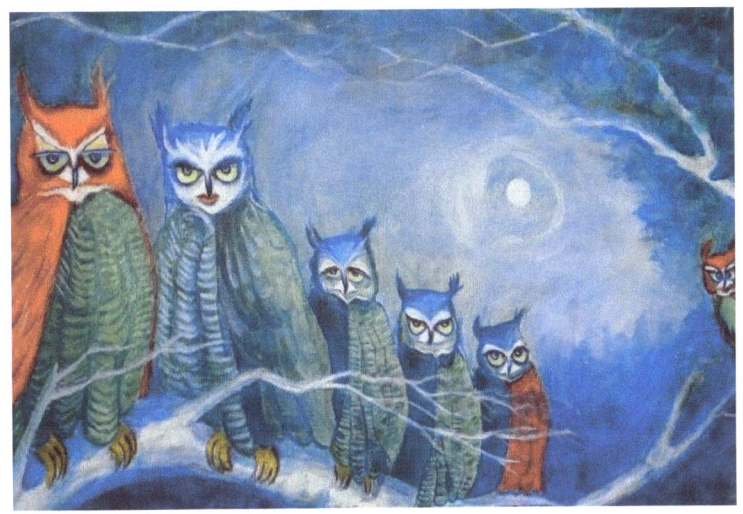

Title: Five or Six Owls
Size: 20x30 inches
Medium: Acrylic on canvas
Copyright by Dan Wetta 1993

This is just a family of owls practicing how to look wise, except for baby owl, who would rather clown around.

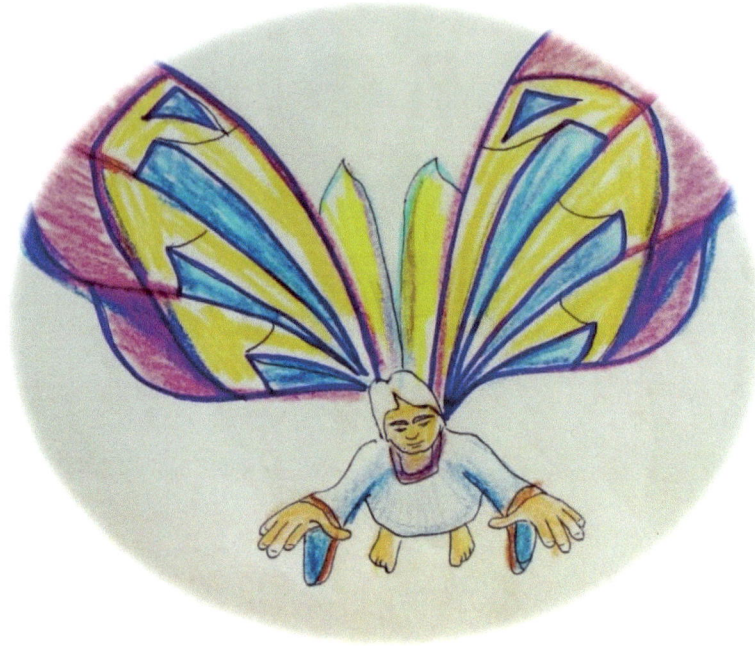

Title: Angel Wings

This is what an angel should look like. An angel like this would feel at home in a stained glass window of any church or even in the window of a cathedral.

Chapter 2: Whacky World

You are now entering the whacky world of Dan Wetta's whacky cartoons.

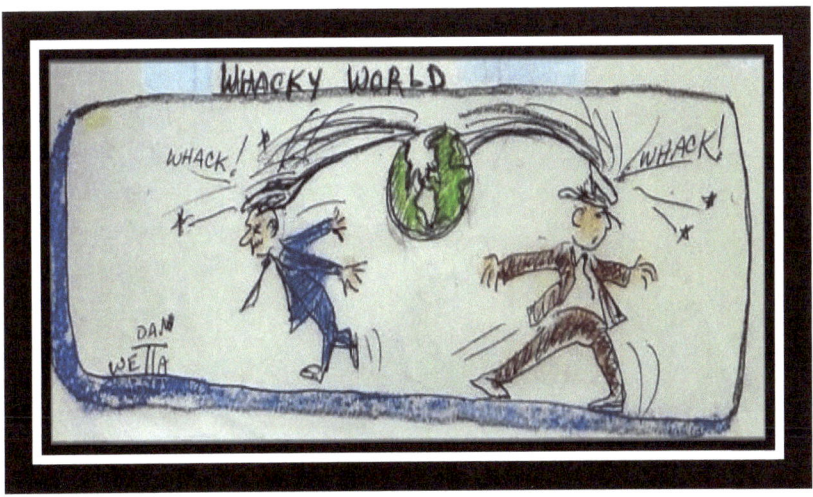

Title: Whacky World cartoon
Copyright by Dan Wetta 1997

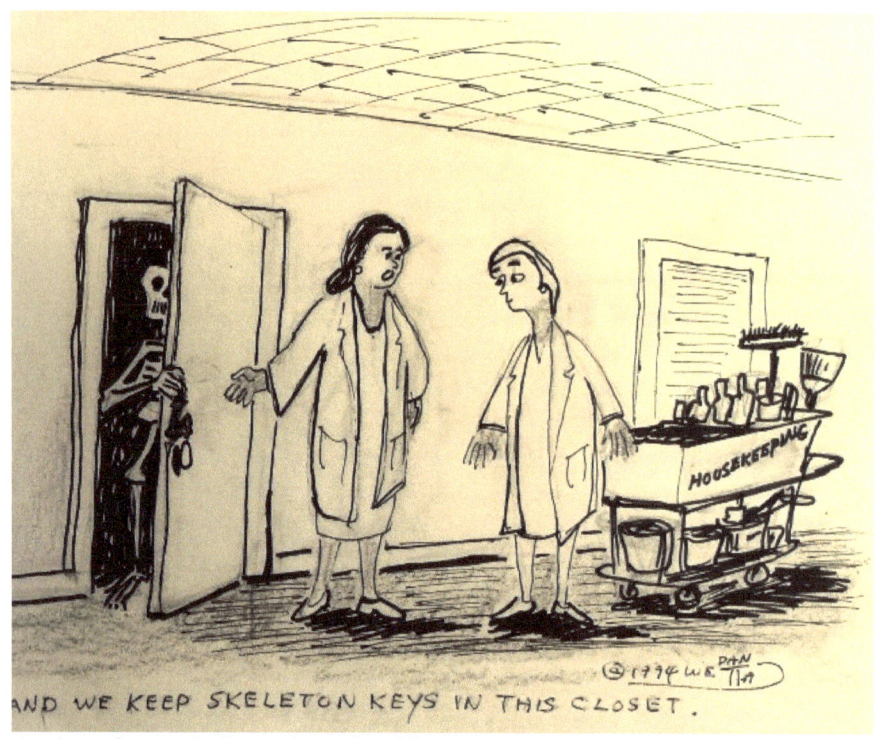

And we keep skeleton keys in this closet!

Title: Skeleton Key Closet
Copyright by Dan Wetta 1994

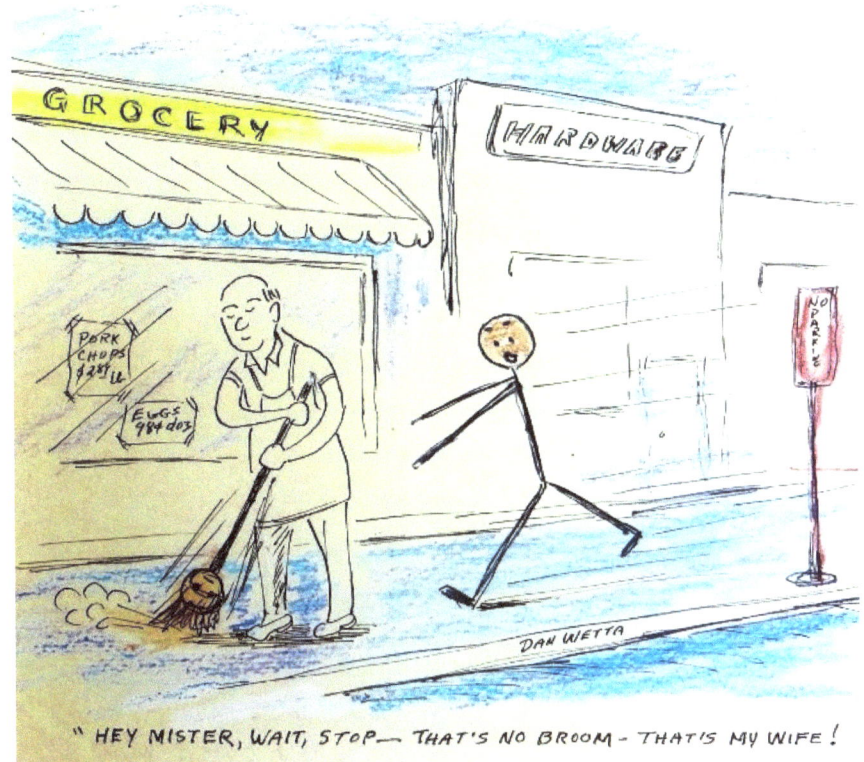

"Hey, Mister, wait, stop! That's no broom! That's my wife!"

Title: That's My Wife
Copyright by Dan Wetta

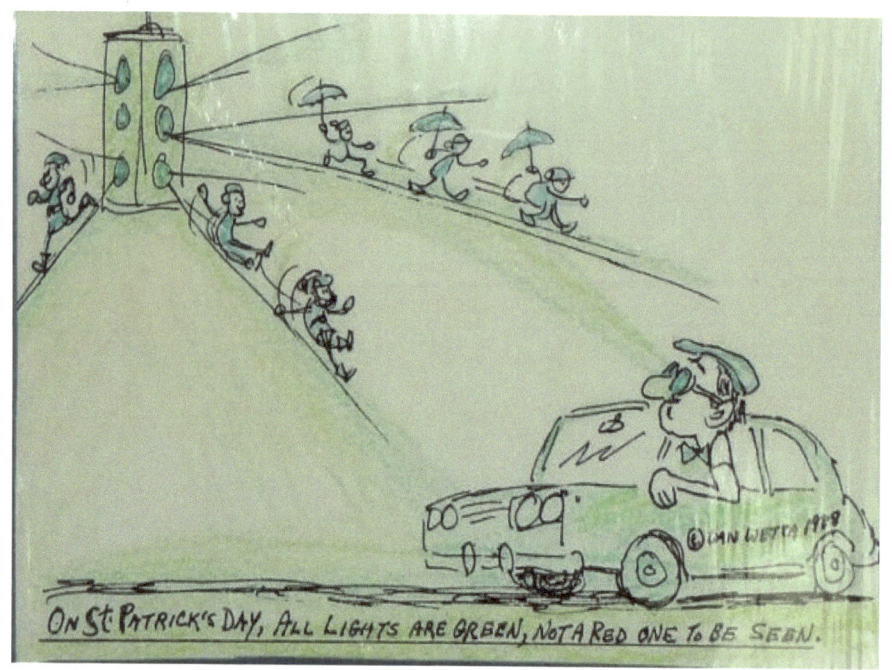

On St. Patrick's Day, all lights are green, not a red one to be seen!

Title: St. Patrick's Day
Copyright Dan Wetta 1989

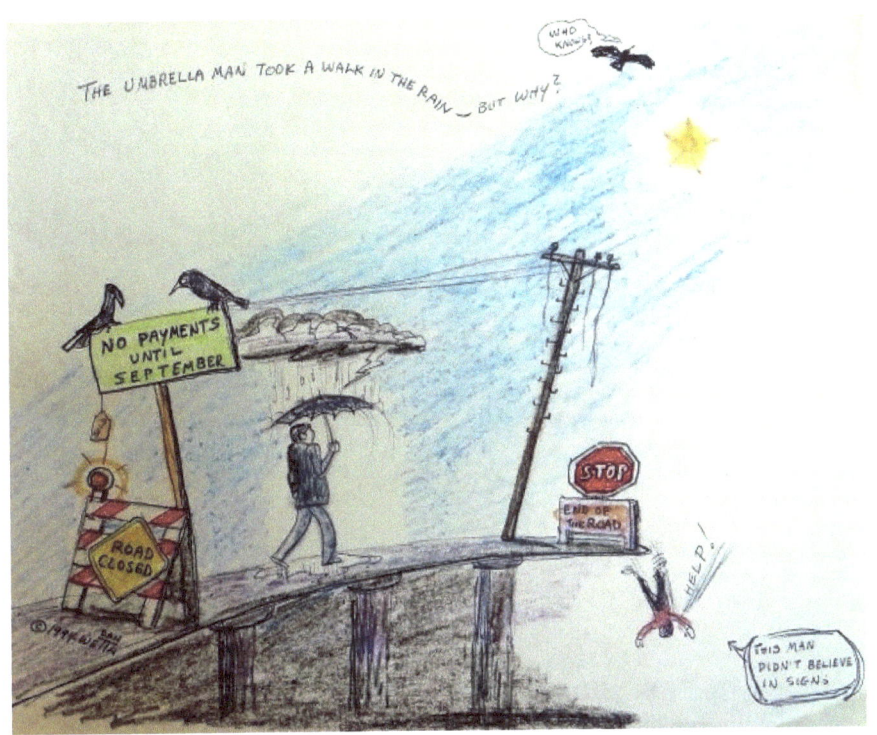

Title: End of the Road
Copyright by Dan Wetta 1994

If this cartoon doesn't make sense, perhaps it's because that sky-writing crow drew it.

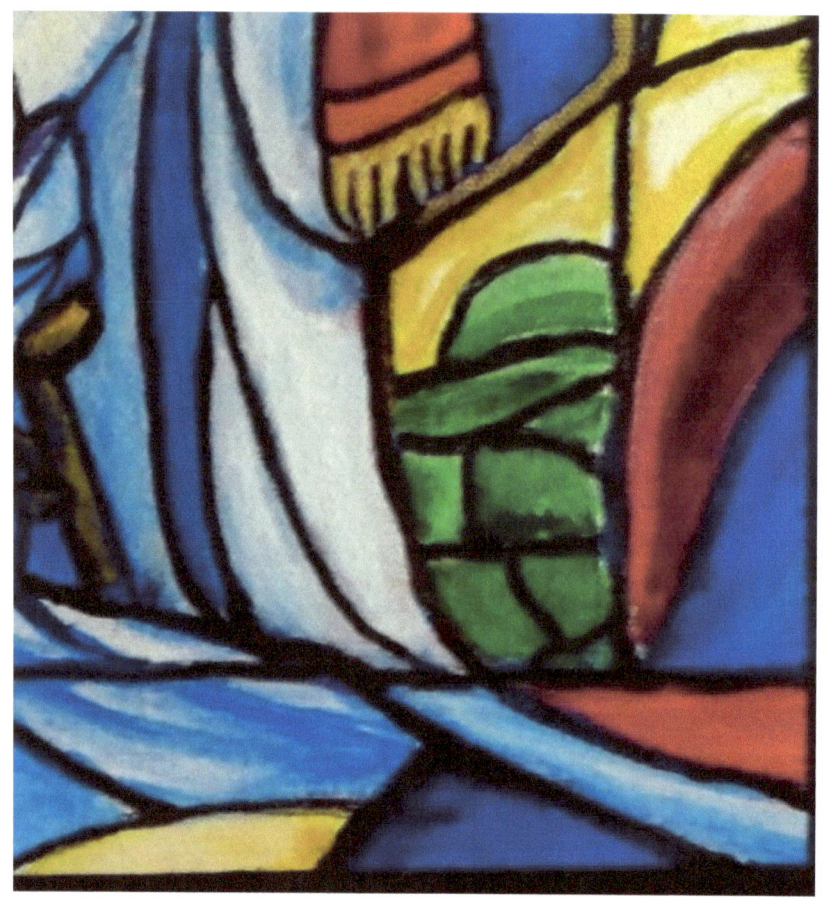

Title: Abstract Nine
Copyright by Dan Wetta

This abstract is taken from "Nativity Scene."

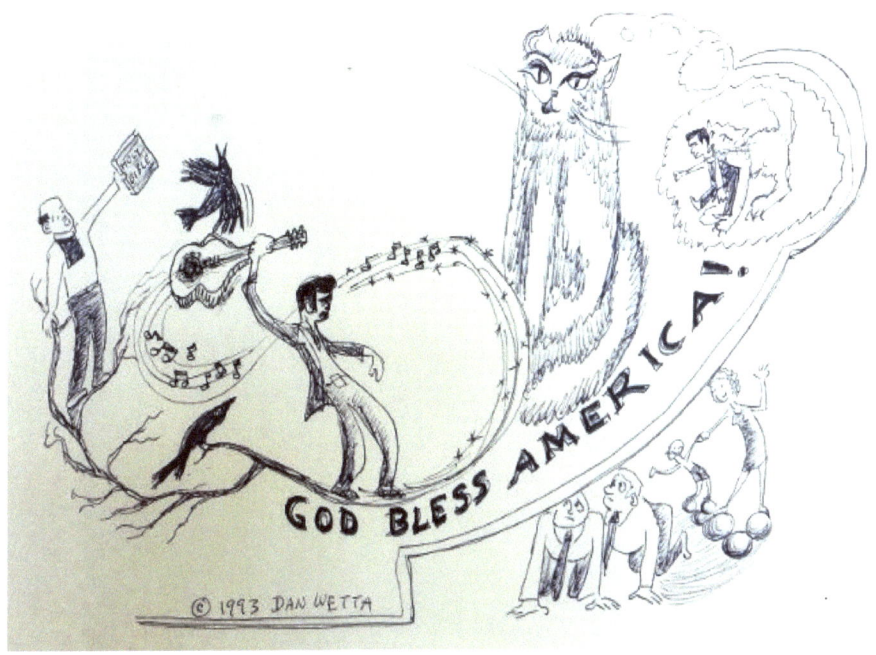

Title: God Bless America
Copyright by Dan Wetta 1993

    With respect to the cartoon, "God Bless America," you're welcome to interpret the cartoon any way you want, depending upon how your brain works. Our interpretation of cartoons, like that of abstract art, can reveal a lot about ourselves.

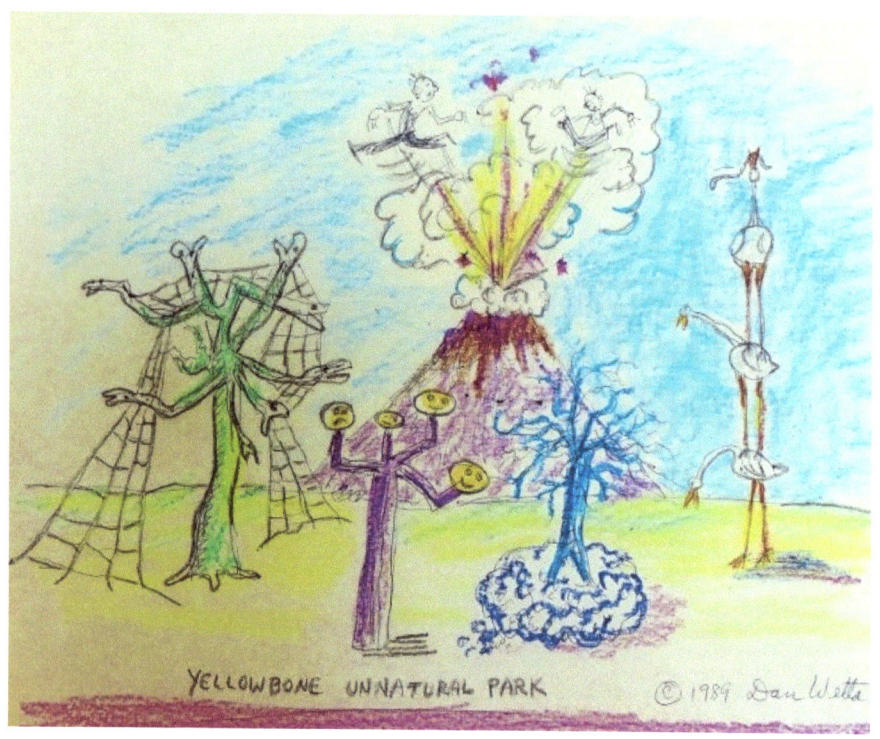

Title: Yellowbone Unnatural Park
Copyright by Dan Wetta 1997

I know some people who actually like to visit places like this.

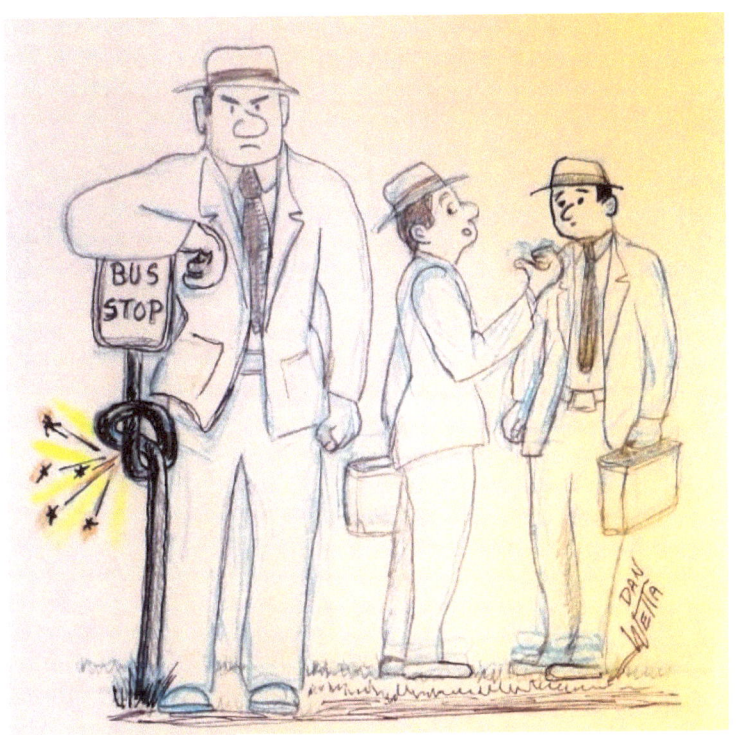

Title: Bad Mood
Copyright by Dan Wetta

"He sure is in a bad mood this morning!"

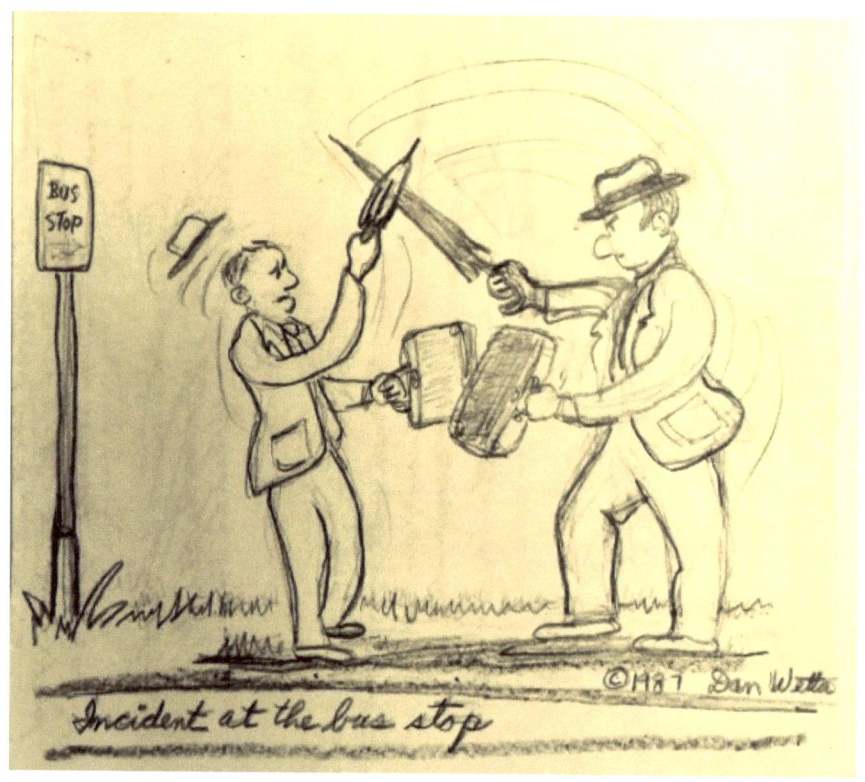

Title: Incident at the Bus Stop
Copyright Dan Wetta 1987

My thoughts would wander when I used to wait for the bus to take me to work in the mornings. One morning, the business brief cases became shields and the umbrellas turned into swords. I only witnessed this duel. I didn't participate.

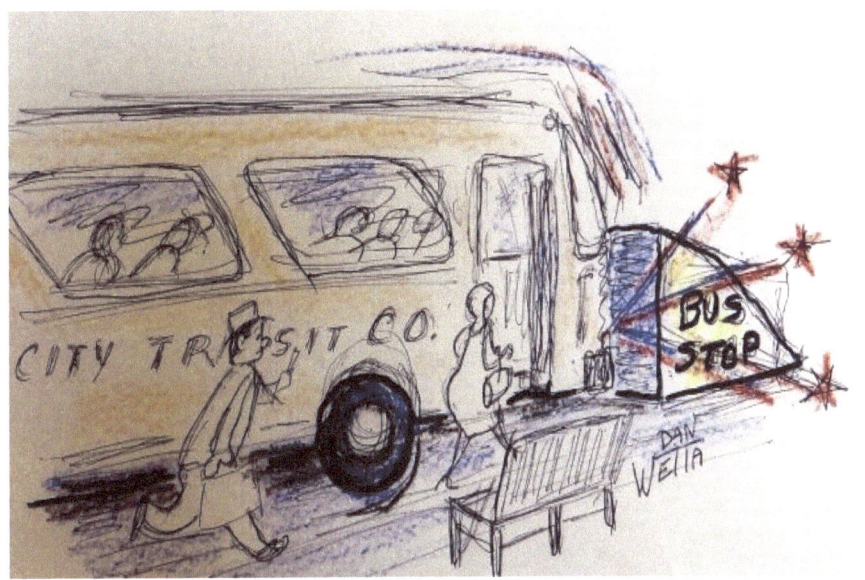

Title: Bus Stop
Copyright Dan Wetta 1987

Every once in a while, when the bus driver was running late, he would not stop for you in the morning, and then you would be late for work. So I invented an automatic bus stop.

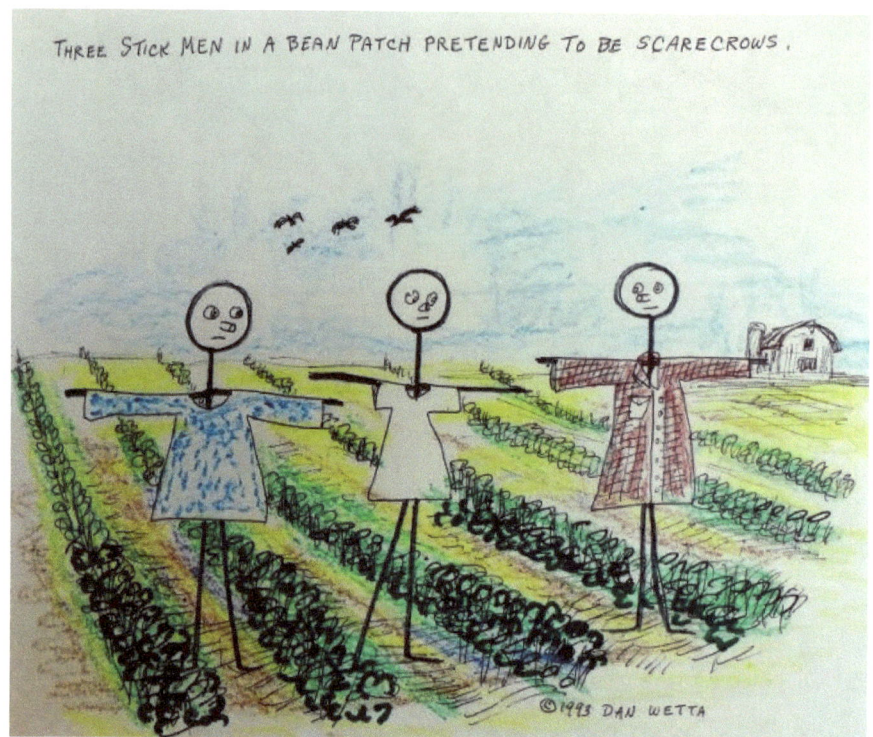

Three stick men in a bean patch pretending to be scarecrows.

Title: Three Stick Men
Copyright Dan Wetta, 1993

As you can see, it's hard to come up with funny stick men gags.

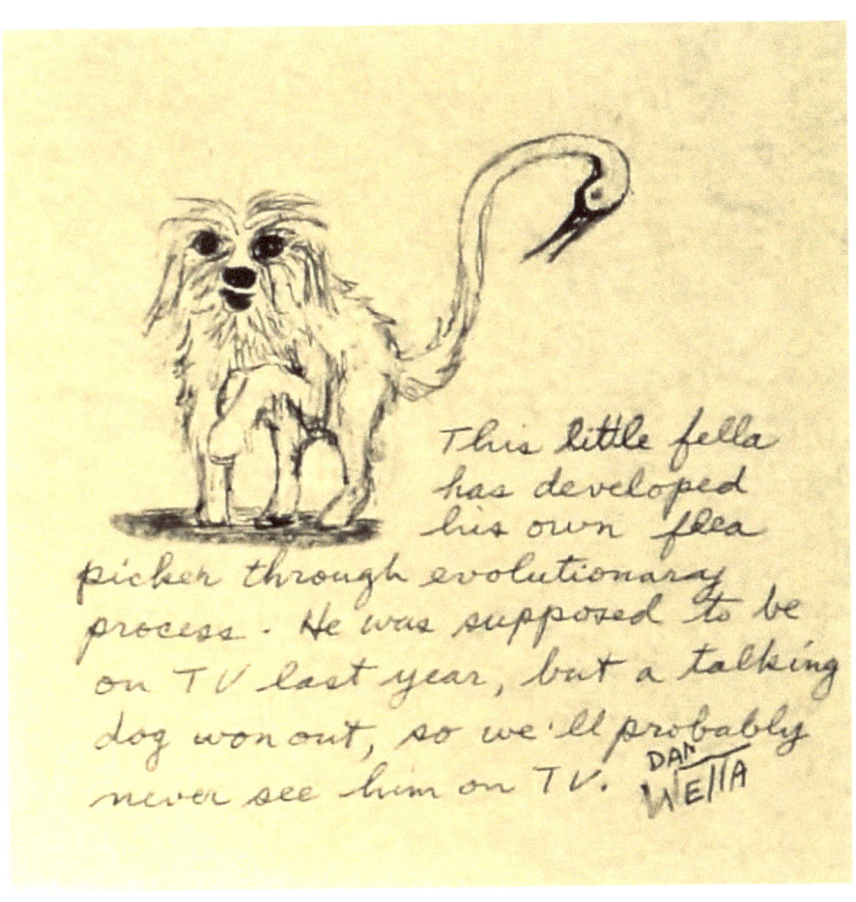

Title: Flea Picker
Copyright by Dan Wetta

How come horse and cow tails evolved into handy fly swatters, but dog tails never developed into flea pickers? That's why I don't believe in evolution.

The cartoon handwriting says, "This little fella has developed his own flea picker through evolutionary process. He was supposed to be on TV last year, but a talking dog won out, so we'll probably never see him on TV."

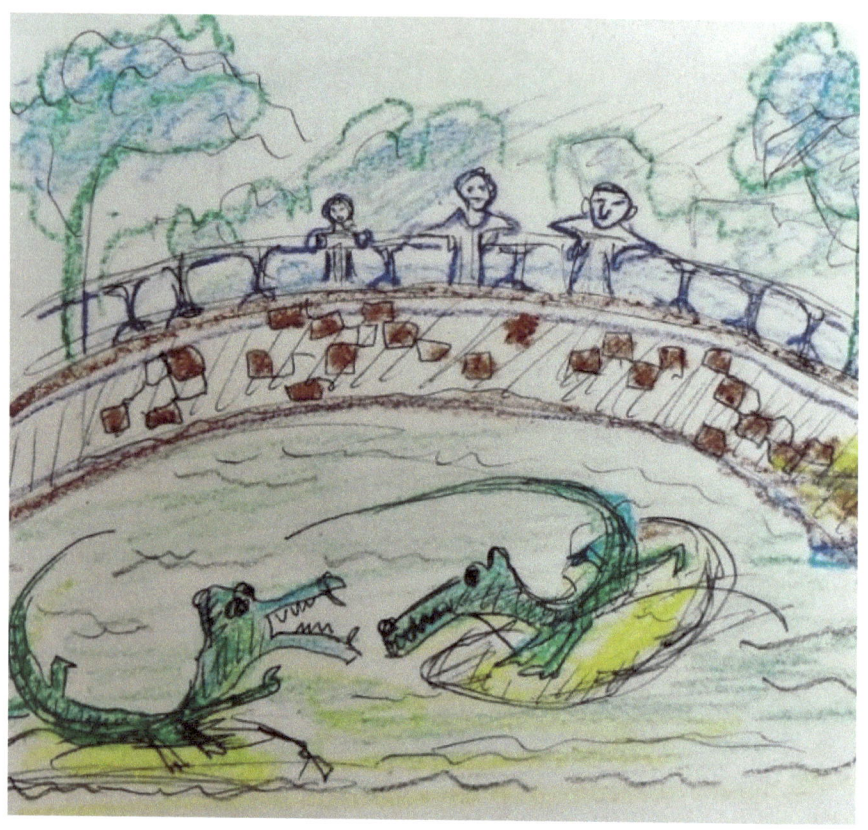

Title: Gator Talk
Copyright by Dan Wetta

    "That's our lunch up there on the bridge. You get the one in the middle, I get the big guy on the end, and whoever finishes first gets the little fellow for a snack."

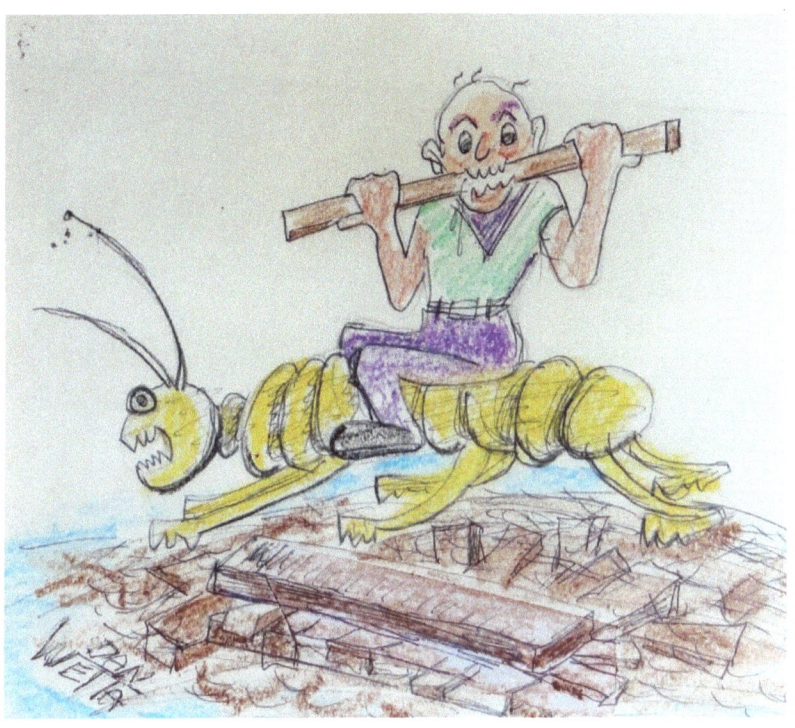

Title: cartoon Termite Man
Copyright by Dan Wetta

    I used to walk a lot. One time when I was walking in a strange neighborhood, I saw a termite man

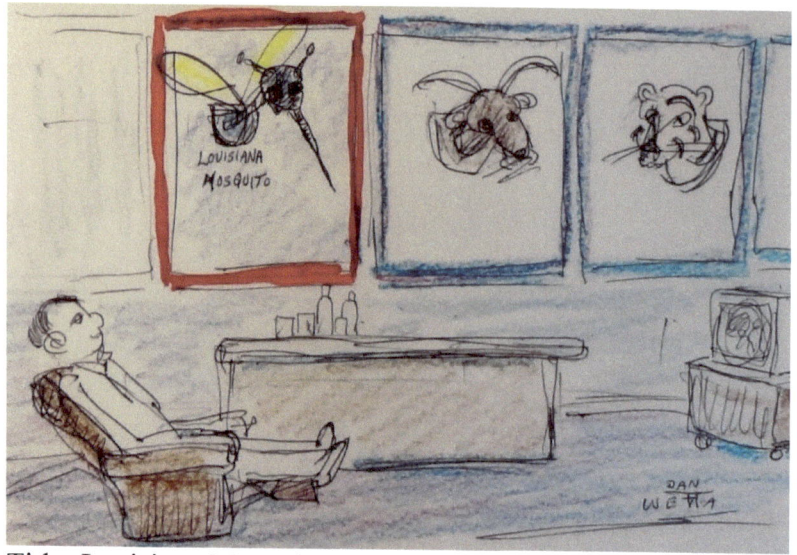

Title: Louisiana Mosquito
Copyright by Dan Wetta

No commentary necessary.

Chapter 3: My Family

Especially my late wife, my granddaughters, and great-grandchildren!

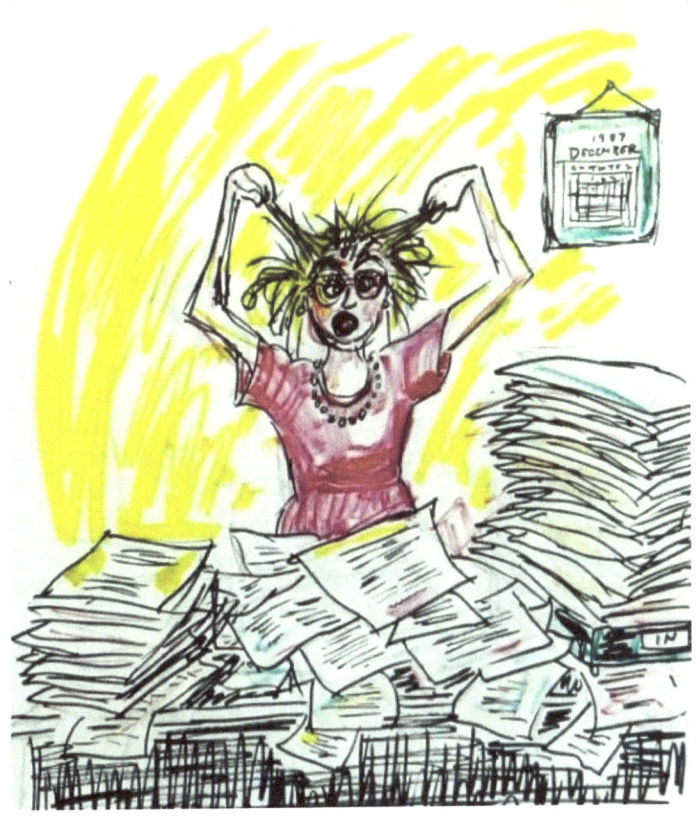

Title Martha at Work 1987
Size: 9"x12"
Medium: Markers on paper
Copyright by Dan Wetta 1987

This is my late wife, Martha, at work just before she retired. But it's not as bad as it looks.

There is a cartoon sequel to this.

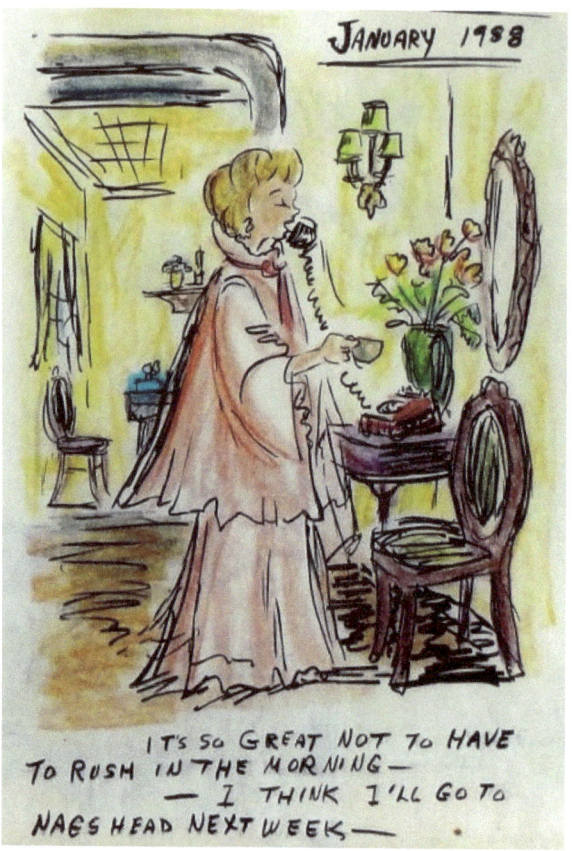

JANUARY 1988

IT's So GREAT NOT To HAVE
TO RUSH IN THE MORNING —
— I THINK I'LL GO TO
NAGS HEAD NEXT WEEK —

Title: Martha Retired
Size: 9x12 inches
Medium: Acrylic on Paper
Copyright 1988 by Dan Wetta

My wife had a good sense of humor. She asked me to do these
two cartoons. In the one above, Martha is retired, and she says on the
phone, "It's so great not to have to rush in the morning - I think I will
go to Nags Head next week." Nags Head is a beach town in the Outer
Banks of North Carolina, where Martha loved to go.

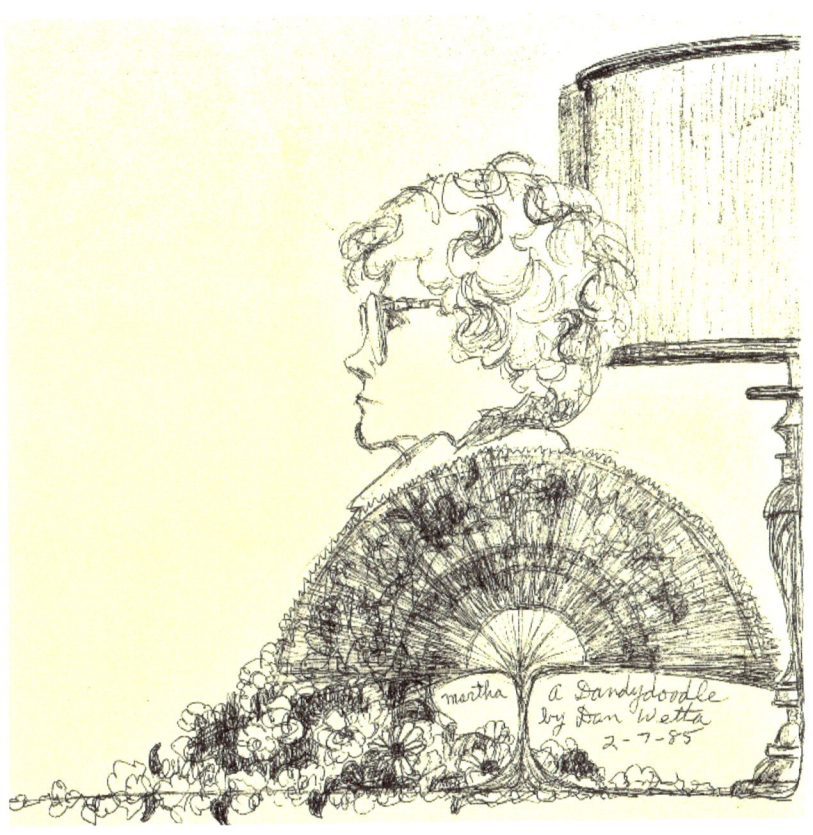

Title: Martha
Copyright by Dan Wetta 1985

Every now and then, I draw a pretty good portrait. This is my late wife, Martha.

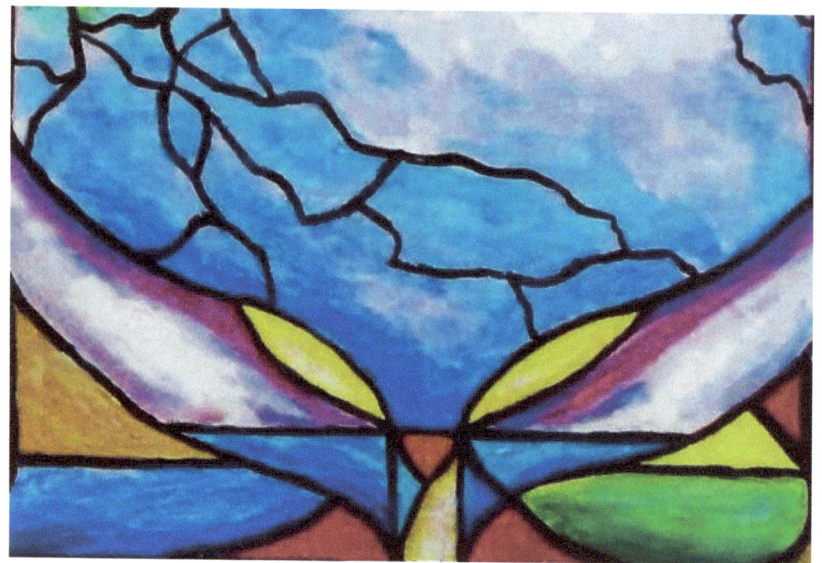

Title: Abstract, Three Panel Garden
Copyright by Dan Wetta

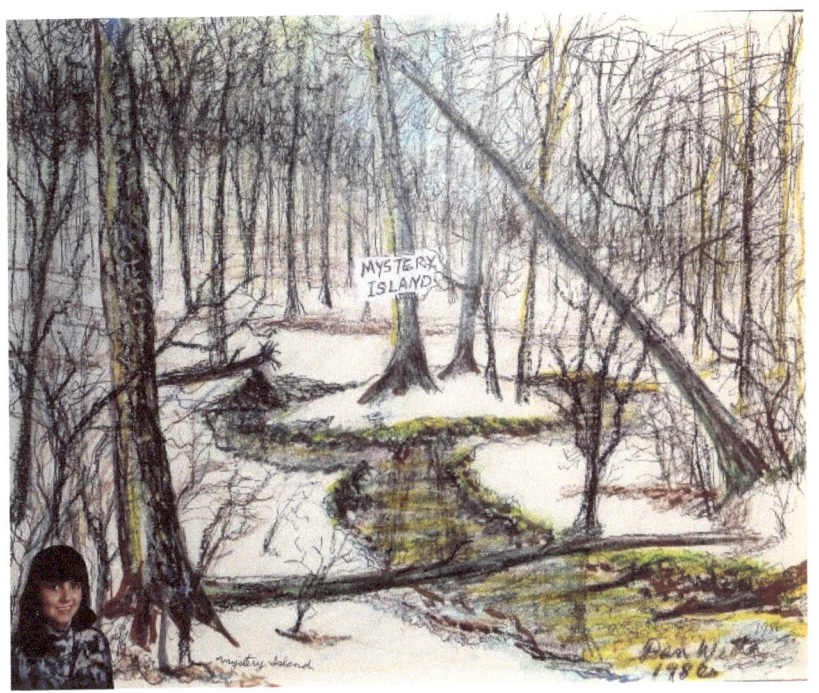

Title: Mystery Island
Size: 12x15 inches
Medium: Mixed media on paper
Copyright by Dan Wetta 1986

My granddaughter, Keira, and the neighborhood kids used to walk past Mystery Island on the way to their secret hideout in the woods.

Actually, Keira does not remember this incident, but I seem to remember that there was an obnoxious ten year old boy who found the secret hideout of Keira and her friends. It overlooked a cow pasture. The boy decided to have some fun with his BB gun. He began peppering the crows with BBs, which caused them to panic because they thought bees were stinging them. The loud crows frightened the cows in the pasture, and so these stampeded. In the chaos of that, the cattle knocked down a fence and trampled a farmer's corn field, soy beans, tomatoes and potatoes.

When harvest time came, the farmer had no crops to sell; therefore, he could not pay the mortgage on the farm. When the bank foreclosed on the house and farm, his wife took their kids and went to live with her mother. The farmer went to the city to look for a job, and, finding none, he wound up living among homeless people. Nobody has heard from him since.

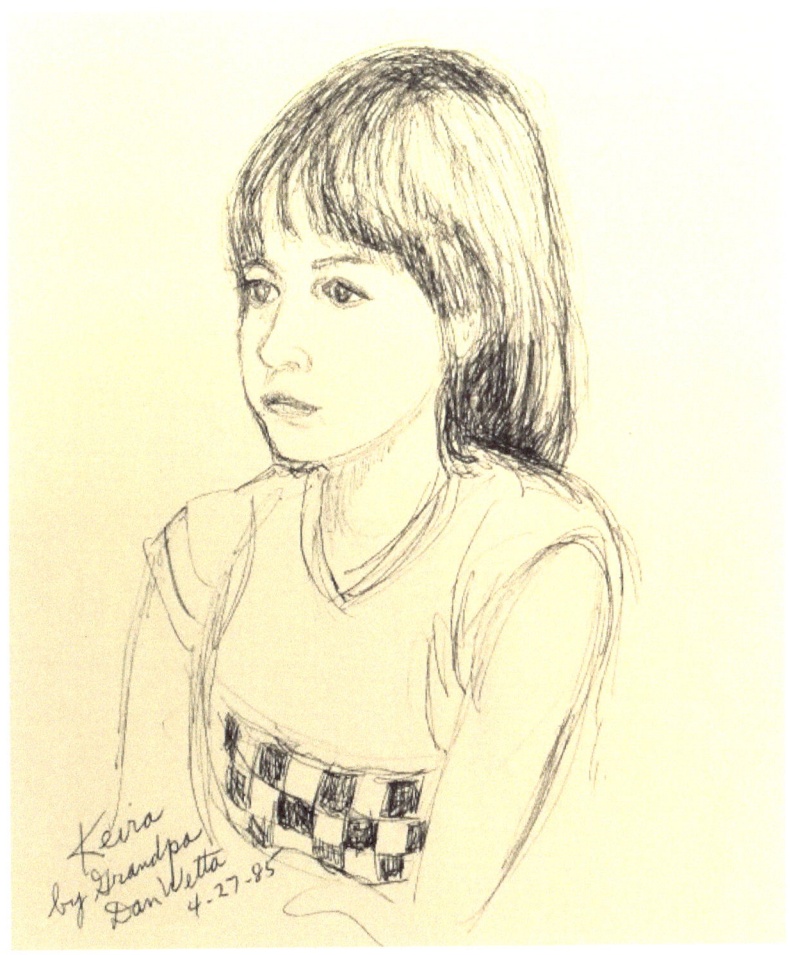

Title: Keira
Copyright by Dan Wetta 1985

As your grandchildren grow up, you grow older.
This is a portrait of my granddaughter, Keira, when she was ten or eleven years old.

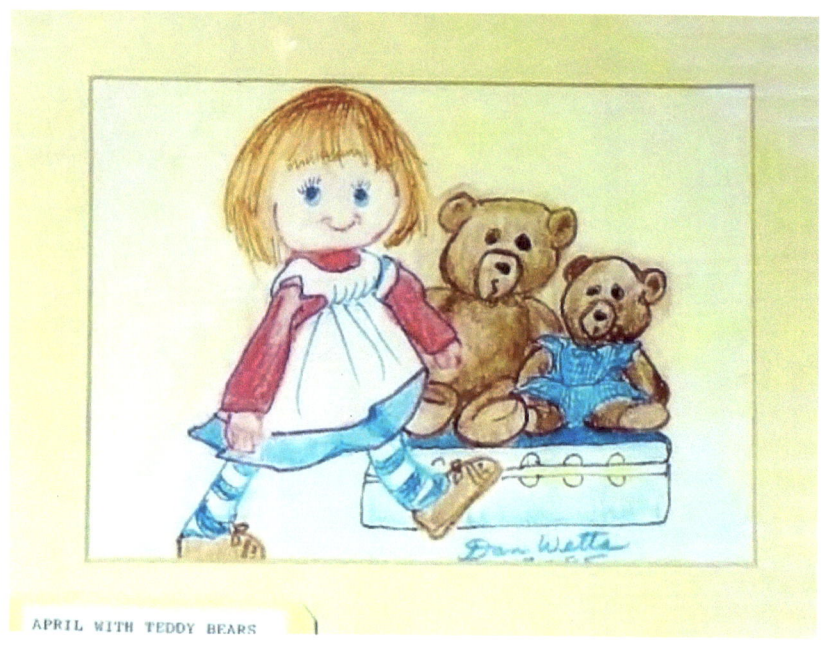

APRIL WITH TEDDY BEARS

Title: April With Teddy Bears
Size: 9x12 inches
Medium: Mixed media on paper
Copyright by Dan Wetta

This is how my granddaughter April used to look when she was about two years old.

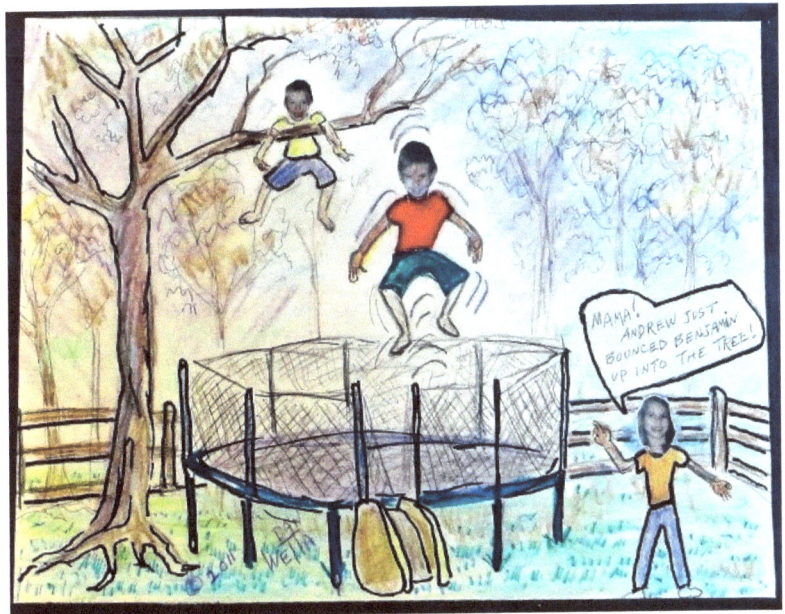

Title: Trampoline
Size: 9x12 inches
Medium: Mixed media on paper
Copyright by Dan Wetta 2011

The talk balloon in this cartoon says it all: "Mama, Andrew just bounced Benjamin up into the tree!"

These are three of my great-grandkids: Benjamin, Andrew, and Maya. Their daddy, Brian, set up a trampoline with a safety net in a corner of the back yard. It kept the kids off the couch and maintained their skinniness. Remember that a safety net is a must for something like this. Yet, even with a safety net, accidents still happen.

The kids had loads of fun and plenty of exercise for three years, until Andrew hit his knee on a metal frame bar, which required a trip to the emergency room for a few stitches.

The parents decided the trampoline was getting old, so they dismantled it.

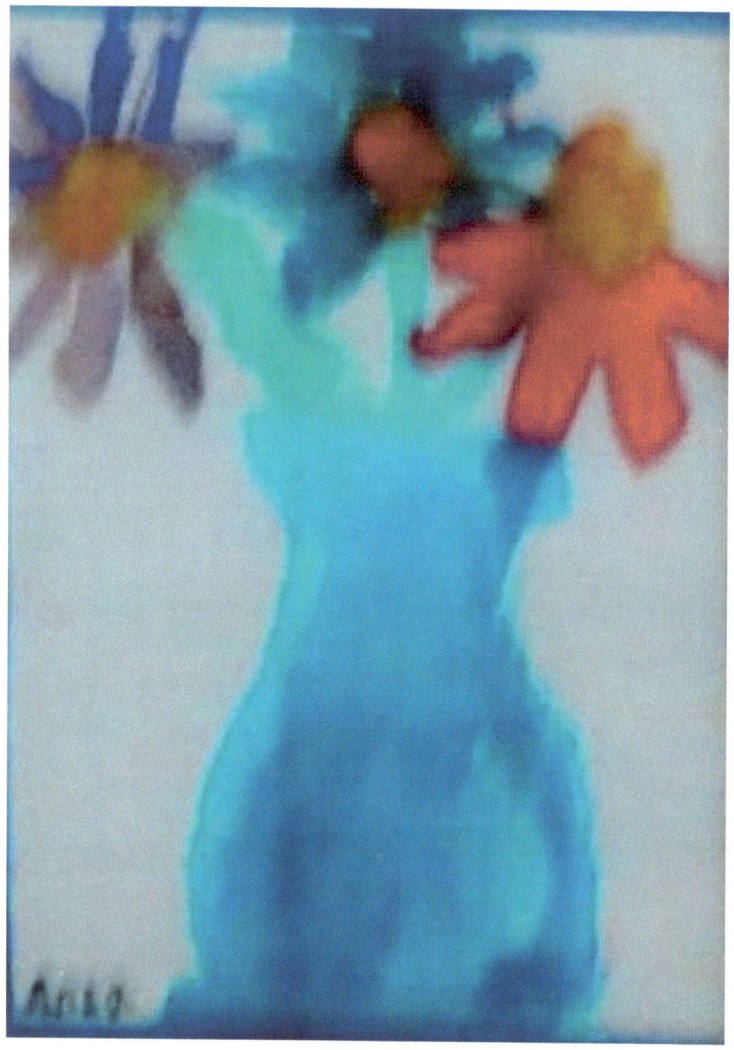

Title: Anna's Vase of Flowers

My great-granddaughter, Anna, painted this vase of flowers when she was about eight years old. She is twelve now and continues to draw and paint, but there is no way to know if she will pursue a career in art or not. Of course, I hope that she will. She currently is taking an art course in her seventh grade class.

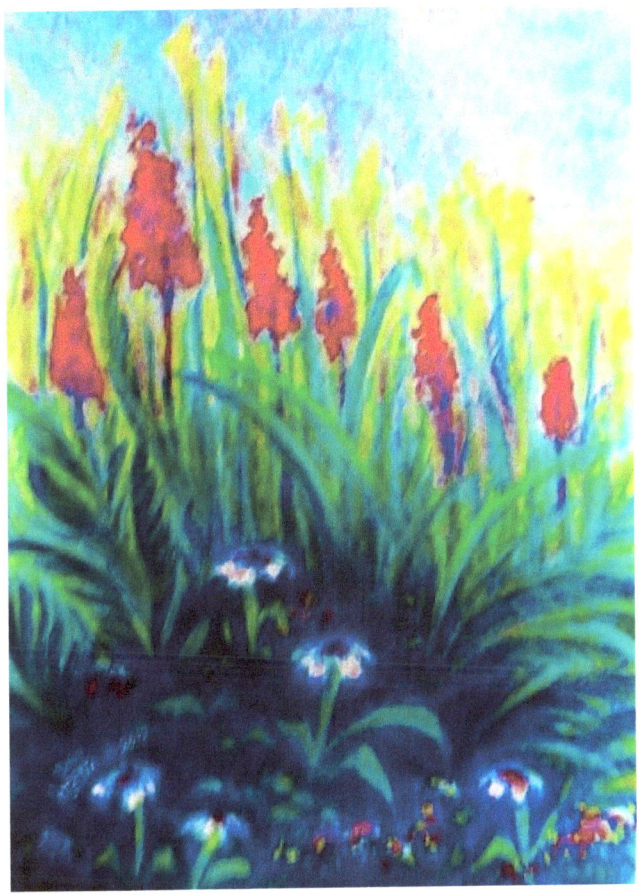

Title: Flowers in Swamp
Size: 18x24 inches
Medium: Acrylic on canvas
Copyright by Dan Wetta 2012

Mother Nature plants flowers everywhere: in the swamps, in the deserts, in the forests. One of my teachers worked for the Civilian Conservation Corps during the Great Depression of the 1930s. She was an artist and lived in a cabin in the woods of Virginia. She recorded the wild flowers of Virginia.

Chapter 4: Odds and Ends

This chapter has a few paintings, anecdotes, cartoons and a warning about the wrong side of the "S-shaped" stream.

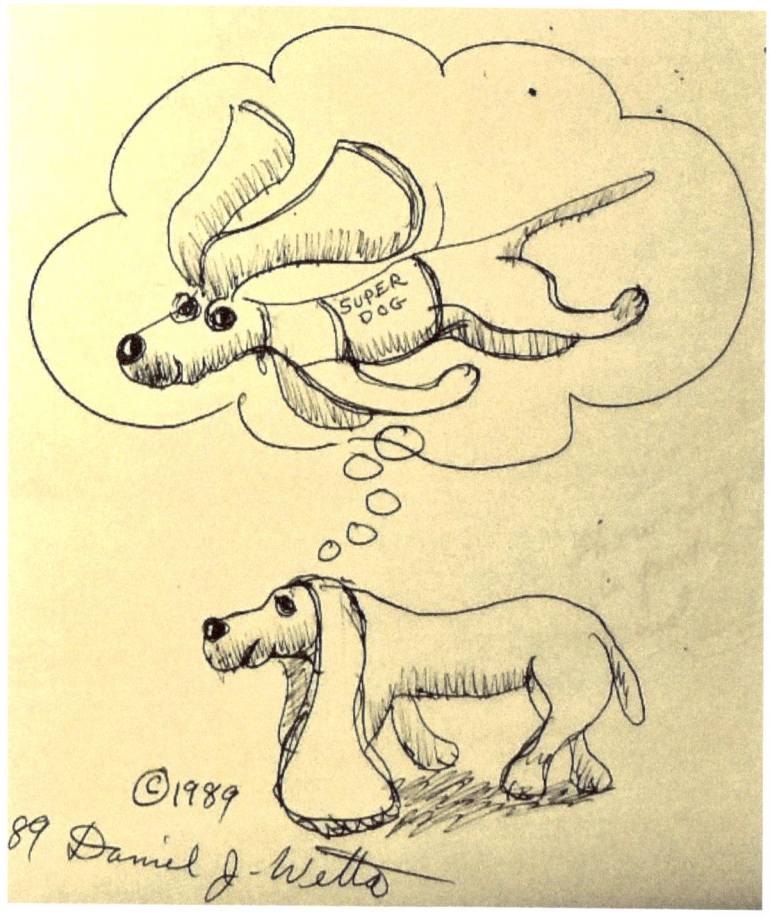

Title: Do Dogs Daydream?
Copyright by Dan Wetta 1989

It is pretty much agreed that dogs dream when they are asleep, so who is to say that they don't daydream?

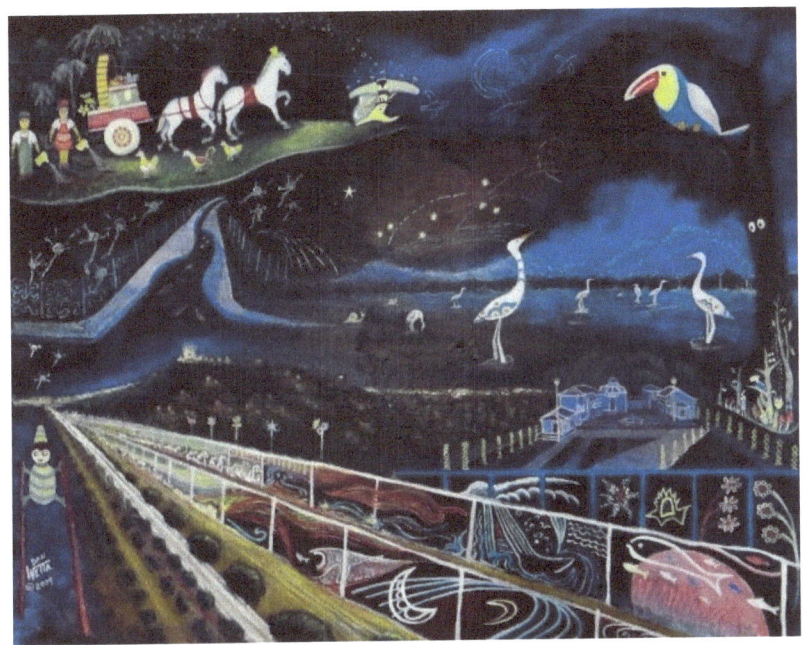

Title: Night Scenes in Medellin, Colombia
Size: 39x49 inches
Medium: Acrylic on canvas
Copyright by Dan Wetta 2009

My Colombian friend, Edith, used to teach me Spanish when she was my neighbor, but she has moved to the countryside. Now we only can get together for lunch about once per month. However, we keep in touch by e-mail. Last year she e-mailed me a lot of night scene photographs from Medellin, Colombia, so I put them together and came up with this painting.

When we were at lunch together recently, I was speaking to Edith in Spanish and she was speaking to me in English.

After about twenty minutes of this, Edith said, "Dan, your Spanish is as bad as my English!"

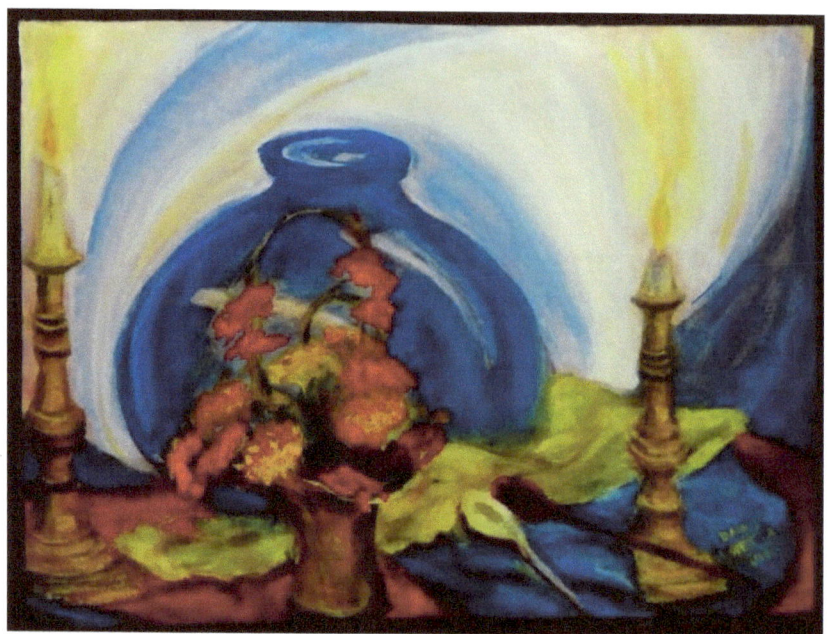

Title: Blue Vase
Size: 18x24 inches
Medium: Acrylic on canvas
Copyright by Dan Wetta 1972

This is different from my normal style of painting because I was taking an art class and I was following the professor's instructions.

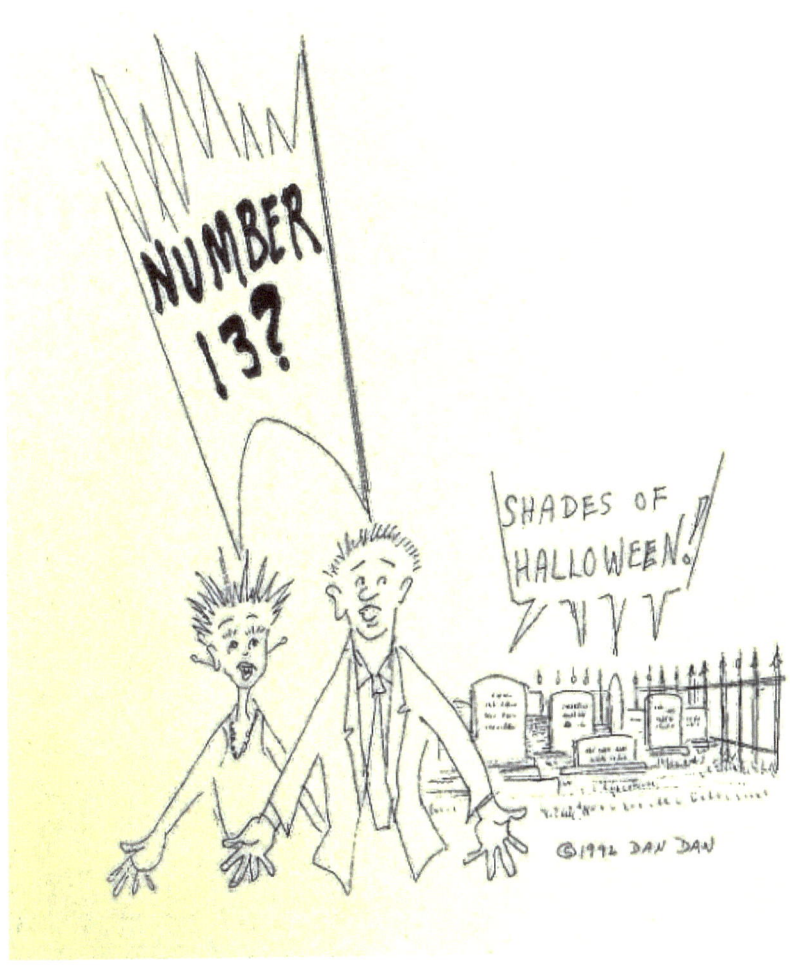

Title: Shades of Halloween
Copyright by Dan Wetta 1992

Superstitions…superstitions!

The next time that you enter an elevator, look at the numbers to see if there is a 13th floor.

I don't remember drawing this cartoon. I just hope that the facial expressions here give you a chuckle.

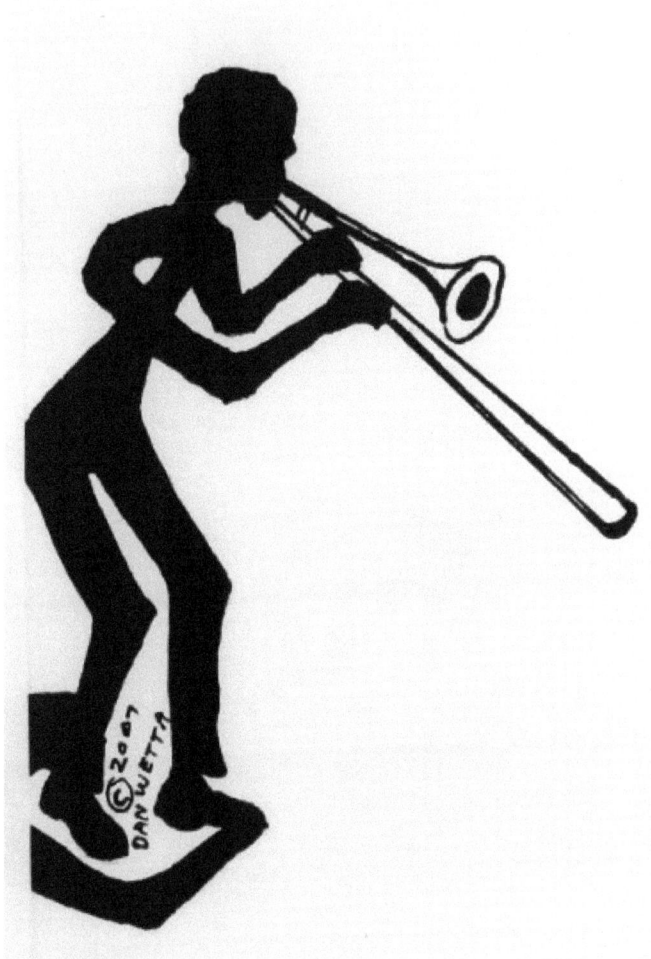

Title: Silhouette Trombone One
Copyright by Dan Wetta 2007

This silhouette is a shadow that has been disconnected from the
trombone player. When you were a kid, did you ever try to run away
from your shadow?

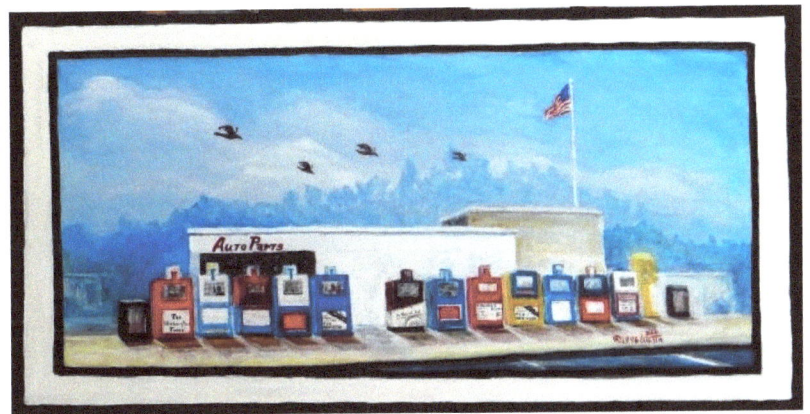

Title: Colorful News
Size: 15x30 inches
Medium: Acrylic on canvas
Copyright by Dan Wetta 1996

The local newspaper is published only twice per week because there is not much news here in Williamsburg, Virginia. But when I saw all those vending machines with newspapers from all over Virginia, Washington and New York, I knew I had to do a painting – but it was the colors of the vending machines that caught my eye, not the news.

When I finished the painting, I thought that there was too much neutral space in the sky, so I added some crows. We have a lot of crows in Williamsburg.

A few years ago, bats began to swoop low over our neighborhood swimming pool in the early evenings. They were trying to catch insects that were hovering above the water. One evening, all of a sudden, a crow zoomed down from seemingly nowhere and captured a bat in its beak!

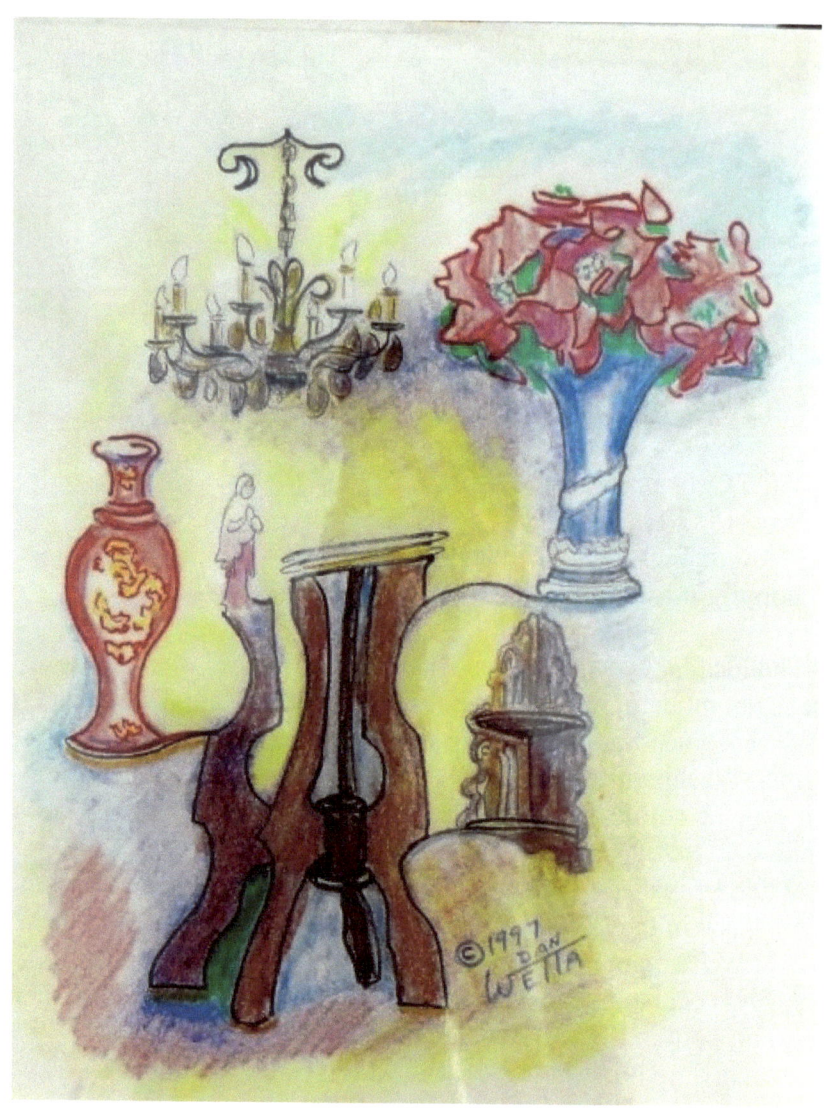

Title: Chandelier and Vase of Flowers
Copyright by Dan Wetta 1997

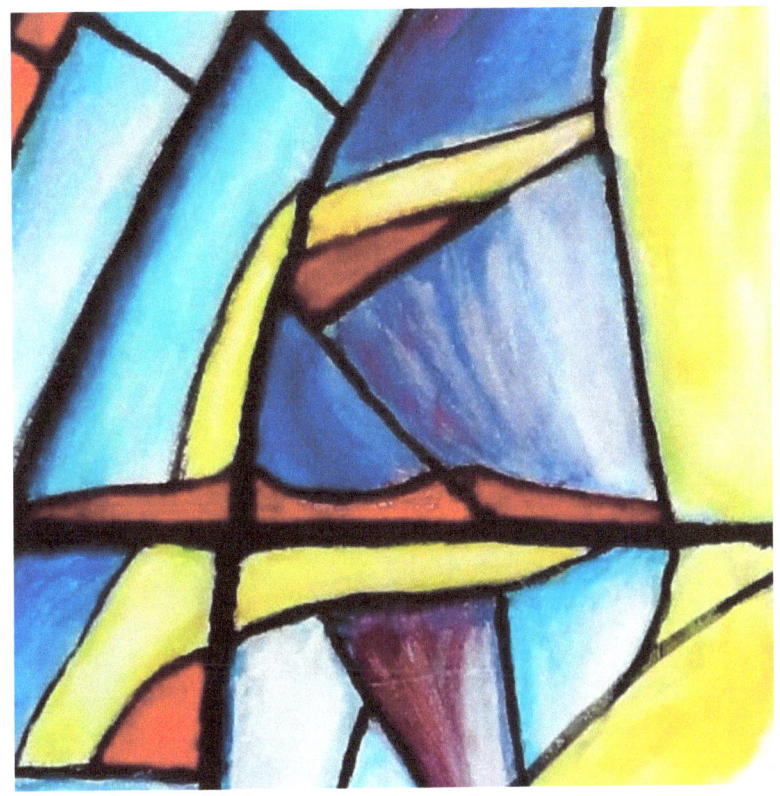

Title: Abstract Eighteen
Copyright by Dan Wetta 1998

This abstract was cropped from my painting, "King Solomon's Verdict."

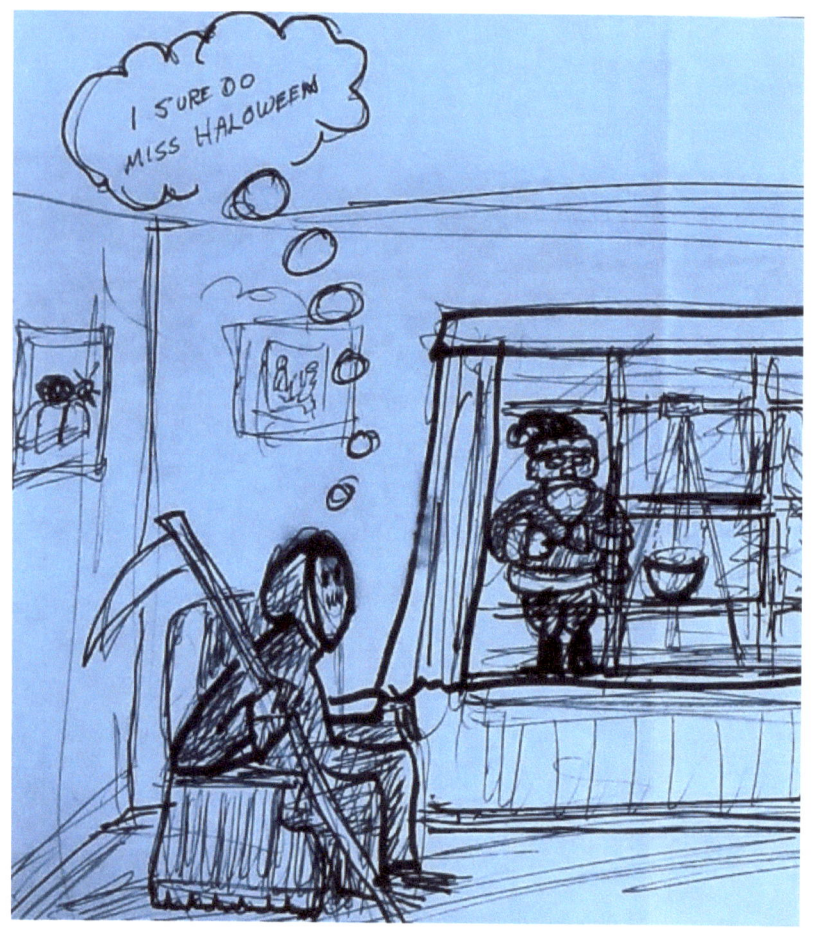

Title: I Miss Halloween
Copyright by Dan Wetta

Even cartoon characters have feelings.

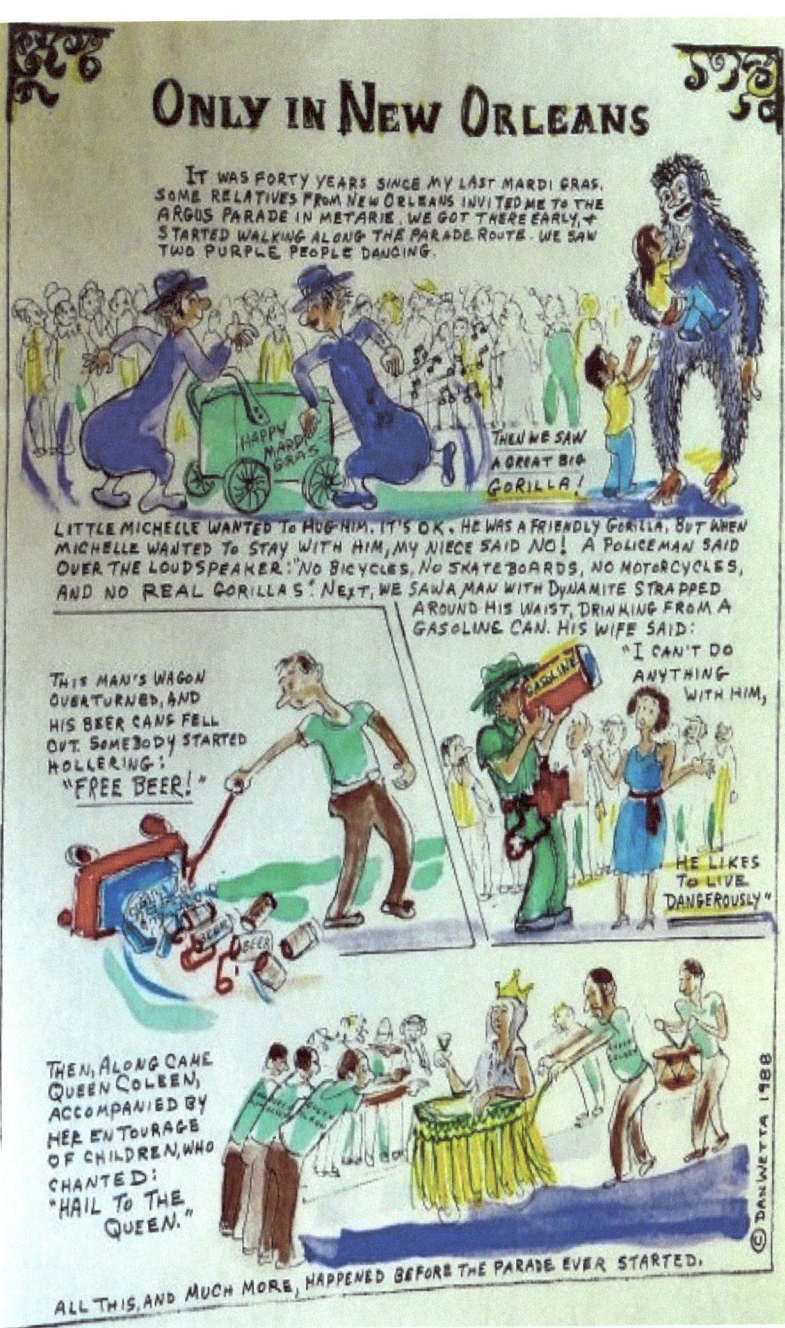

ONLY IN NEW ORLEANS

IT WAS FORTY YEARS SINCE MY LAST MARDI GRAS. SOME RELATIVES FROM NEW ORLEANS INVITED ME TO THE ARGUS PARADE IN METARIE. WE GOT THERE EARLY, & STARTED WALKING ALONG THE PARADE ROUTE. WE SAW TWO PURPLE PEOPLE DANCING.

THEN WE SAW A GREAT BIG GORILLA!

LITTLE MICHELLE WANTED TO HUG HIM. IT'S OK. HE WAS A FRIENDLY GORILLA, BUT WHEN MICHELLE WANTED TO STAY WITH HIM, MY NIECE SAID NO! A POLICEMAN SAID OVER THE LOUDSPEAKER:"NO BICYCLES, NO SKATEBOARDS, NO MOTORCYCLES, AND NO REAL GORILLAS! NEXT, WE SAW A MAN WITH DYNAMITE STRAPPED AROUND HIS WAIST, DRINKING FROM A GASOLINE CAN. HIS WIFE SAID:

THIS MAN'S WAGON OVERTURNED, AND HIS BEER CANS FELL OUT. SOMEBODY STARTED HOLLERING: "FREE BEER!"

"I CAN'T DO ANYTHING WITH HIM, HE LIKES TO LIVE DANGEROUSLY"

THEN, ALONG CAME QUEEN COLEEN, ACCOMPANIED BY HER ENTOURAGE OF CHILDREN, WHO CHANTED: "HAIL TO THE QUEEN."

ALL THIS, AND MUCH MORE, HAPPENED BEFORE THE PARADE EVER STARTED.

© DANWETTA 1988

Title: Only in New Orleans
Copyright by Dan Wetta 1988

This cartoon tells the story of Mardi Gras, which I have not attended in more than forty years. In New Orleans, Mardi Gras has a series of parades over the course of a week. Some are sponsored and some are "neighborhood parades."

Neighborhood parades like this are for the kids and are more fun than the professional tourist parades during Mardi Gras season.

My cartoon above ends with an illustration of how Coleen's sons honor her as a queen in one of these neighborhood parades.

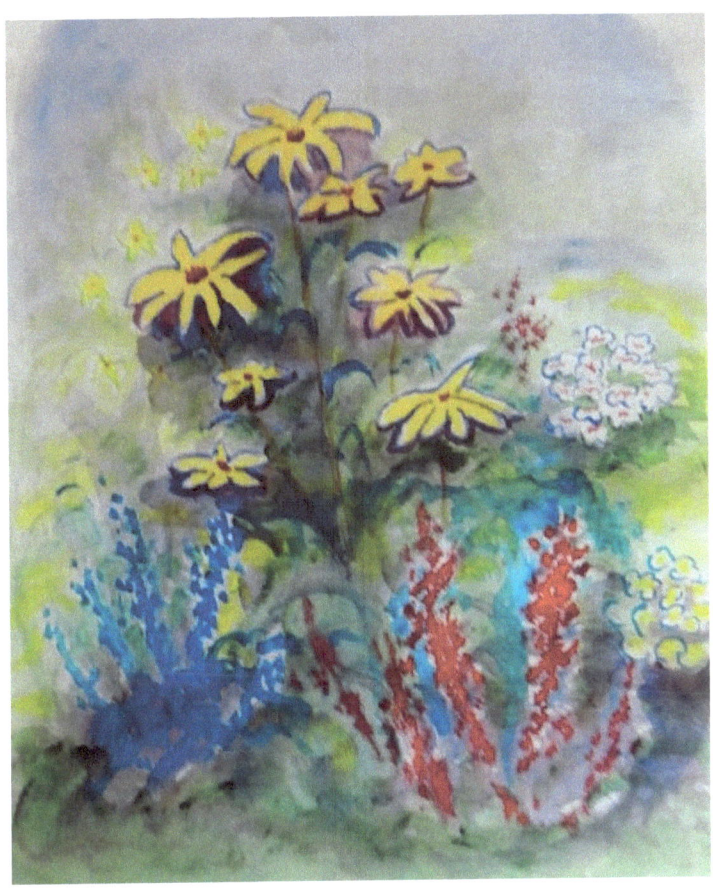

Title: Red, Yellow and Blue Flowers
Size: 16x20 inches
Medium: Acrylic on paper
Copyright by Dan Wetta

I saw these flowers in a tiny garden by the corner of my neighbor Faye's condo. Faye grew up in the original Colonial Williamsburg before it was restored by the Rockefeller Foundation. I think her home was near the Palace Green.

Faye was a genteel southern lady. She lived 93 years. We should all live that long.

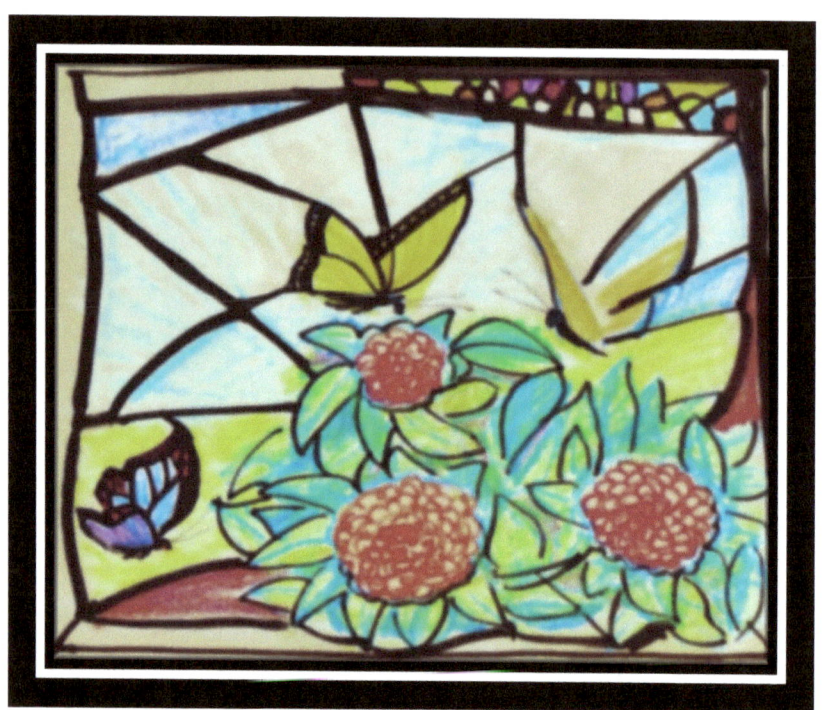

Title: Butterfly Flowers
Medium: Mixed media on paper

This is just a butterfly doodle – three butterflies and three flowers, plenty to go around.

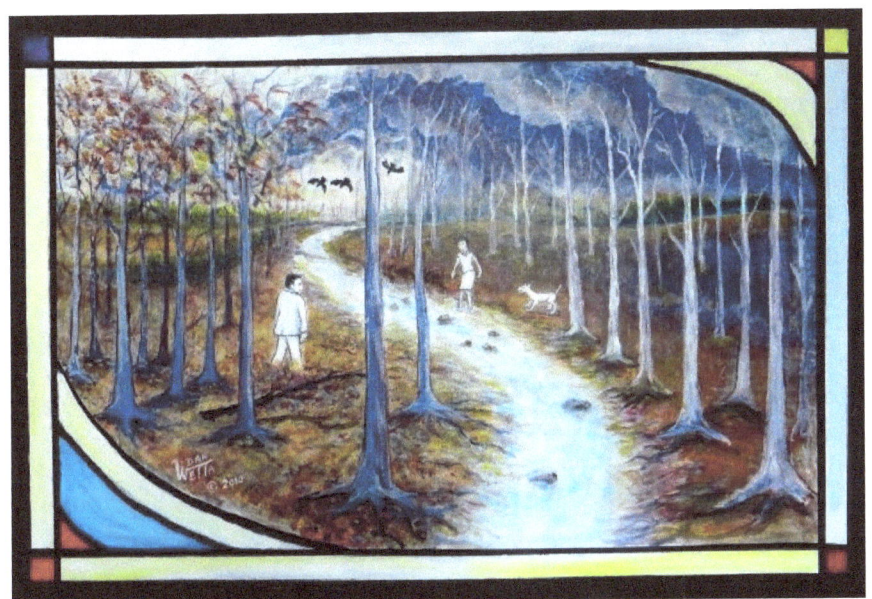

Title: S-Stream
Size: 24x36 inches
Medium: Acrylic on canvas
Copyright by Dan Wetta 2010

"How to draw" books will tell you that a path, road or stream in the woods will look better if you give it an "S" shape. However, they do not mention that there is a good side and a bad side to the "S" shape.

My granddaughter, Keira, thinks that this painting is weird…and so it is…because the man and his wife inadvertently crossed over to the wrong side of the stream. They turned back immediately when they noticed that all the trees were white because the sap had been drained from them.

Keira said that the man in the painting looks like Frankenstein, but that is because he has just crossed back to the good side of the stream and has not returned to normal yet. He is trying to coax his wife to come over to him, but she is frozen with fear and cannot move. Their dog is barking encouragement to her.

Those crows flying above the stream dare not venture into the eerie woods because they would turn white with fear. Whoever heard of a white crow?

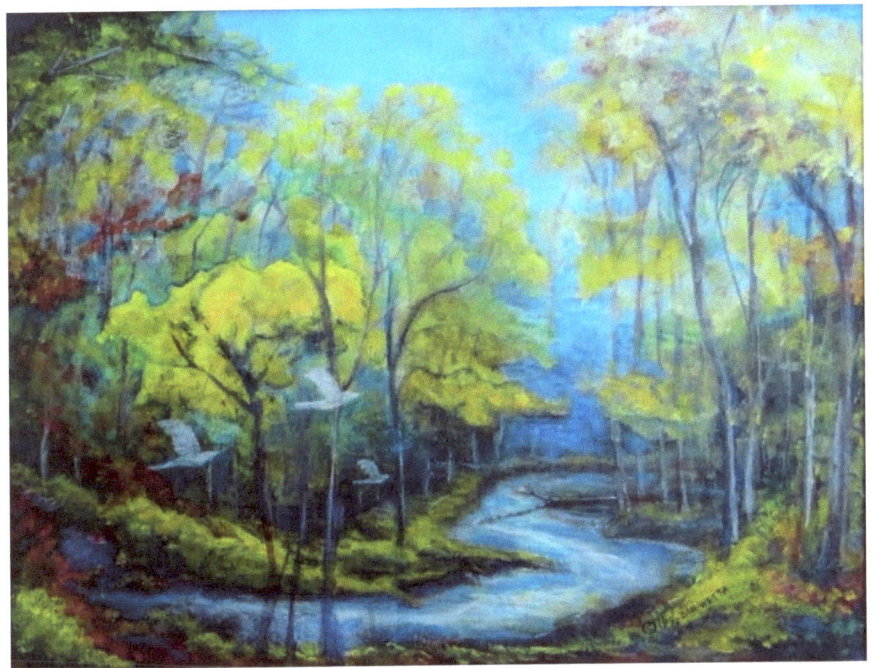

Title: S-Stream, Enchanted Wood
Size: 20x30 inches
Medium: Acrylic on canvas
Copyright by Dan Wetta 1995

If you go for a walk in the woods, go into the Enchanted Wood, where all is well on both sides of the S-stream.

Chapter 5: Some Memories to Share

While I was earning a living as an auditor/ accountant, my life would have been pretty boring and humdrum if it had not been for my avocation: art.

I have been drawing, painting and cartooning ever since I was a child. So whenever I returned to Louisiana from Virginia to visit relatives, I always came home with sketches or snapshots of the South, and, occasionally, I would draw a cartoon when I was reminiscing about something that happened when I was a kid in New Orleans, such as the time a rat bit my daddy's toe after he fell asleep on the sofa.

So I hope you will find this chapter to be an interesting and, perhaps, hilarious account of the life of a bookkeeper.

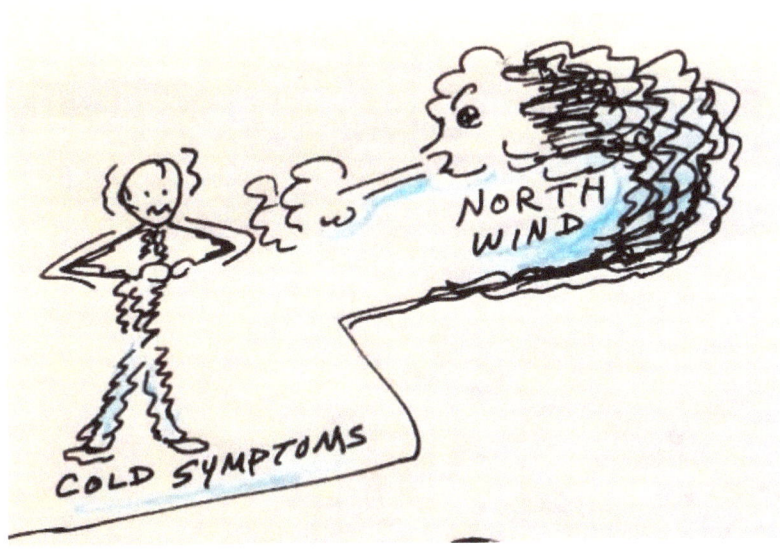

Title: I'm Always Freezing

I enlisted in the Army in October, 1946, and they transported us from hot Louisiana to Fort Sam, Houston, Texas, where it was close to 100 degrees. A couple of days later, they put us on a train, and, on my birthday, October 10th, we arrived at Camp Lee, Virginia, where it was very cold.

I was assigned to a tar-paper barracks with only one wood stove in the middle of the barracks for heat. My bunk was at the front door, which was opening and closing continually as the guys came in and out of the barracks.

The latrine was a hundred yards away, and we had to shave with cold water.

I have been freezing cold ever since!

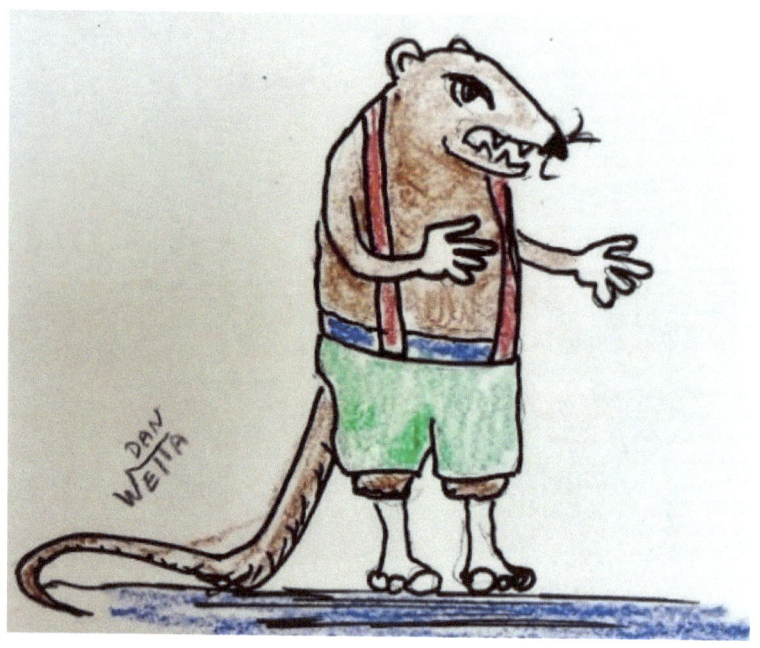

Title: The Rat That Bit My Daddy's Toe!
Copyright by Dan Wetta

During the 1930's, when I was a kid in New Orleans, my dad used to fall asleep while reading the newspaper on the sofa. One night we all went to bed upstairs, but we didn't wake Daddy up because he was sound asleep.

The next morning, Daddy complained that a rat bit his toe and woke him up during the night. From that time on, my father would refer to anybody whom he didn't like as a "dirty rat." That's how the expression, "dirty rat," was coined. At least, I thought so!

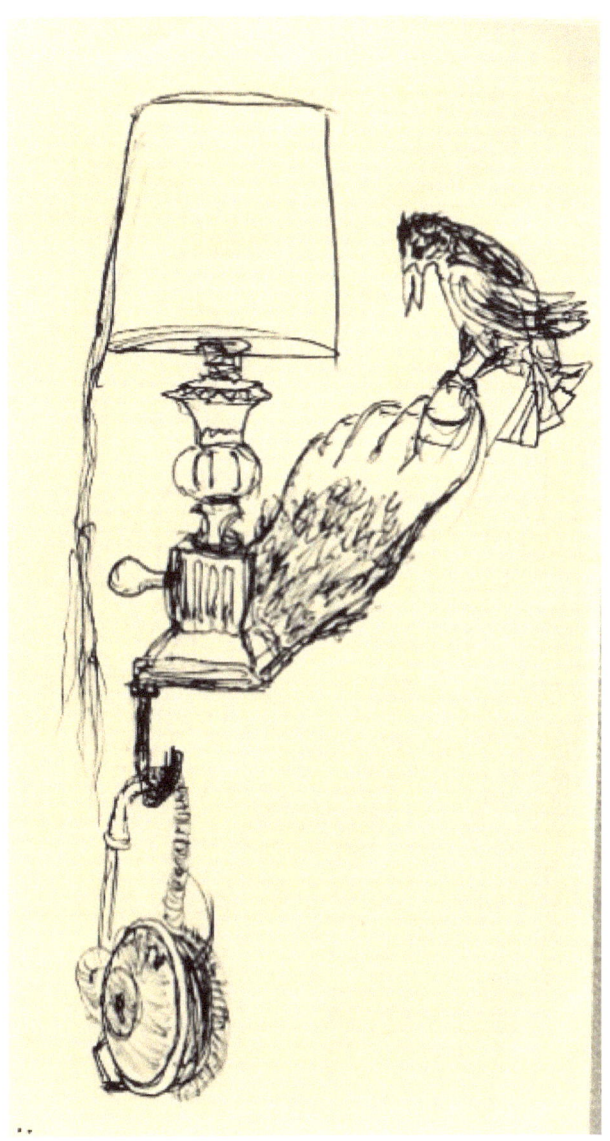

Title: Crow on a Toe
Copyright by Dan Wetta

Doodles do not always make good sense, but doodles are doodles.

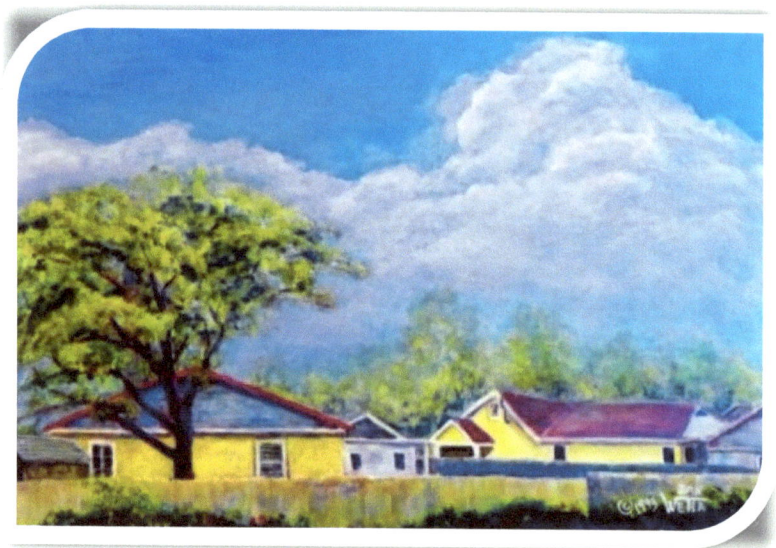

Title: Backyard Harahan
Size: 20x30 inches
Medium: Acrylic on canvas
Copyright by Dan Wetta 1993

This is the back yard of my brother, Urban, who used to live next door to my sister, Anna Marie, in Harahan, Louisiana.

During Hurricane Katrina in 2005, Anna Marie and her husband sought shelter at Ochsner Clinic, where their daughter, Marcelle, was on nursing duty. However, conditions at the clinic deteriorated so badly that Anna Marie felt like they would be better off at home.

So she asked Urban to come get them. He was able to rescue and drive them home through flooded streets and marauding mobs.

They managed to do okay at home, even though there was no electricity or running water for a few weeks after the storm.

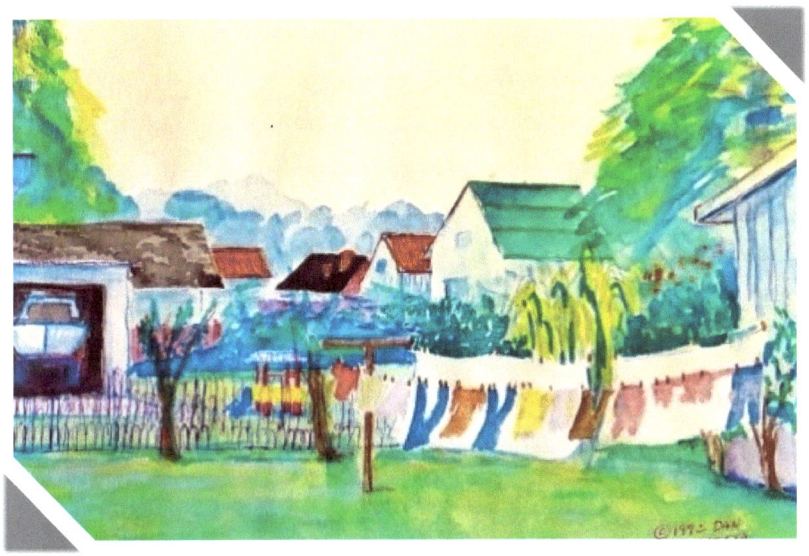

Title: Anna Marie's Clothes Line
Size: 13 x 18 inches
Medium: Mixed media on paper
Copyright by Dan Wetta 1992

My sister still hangs her clothes out to dry, and they dry rapidly under the hot Louisiana sun.

We always carried an umbrella when we walked to the grocery store to shade us from the sweltering Louisiana sun. It is still a common sight in Louisiana to see people carrying umbrellas to shield themselves from the merciless sunlight.

Hot, hot, hot!

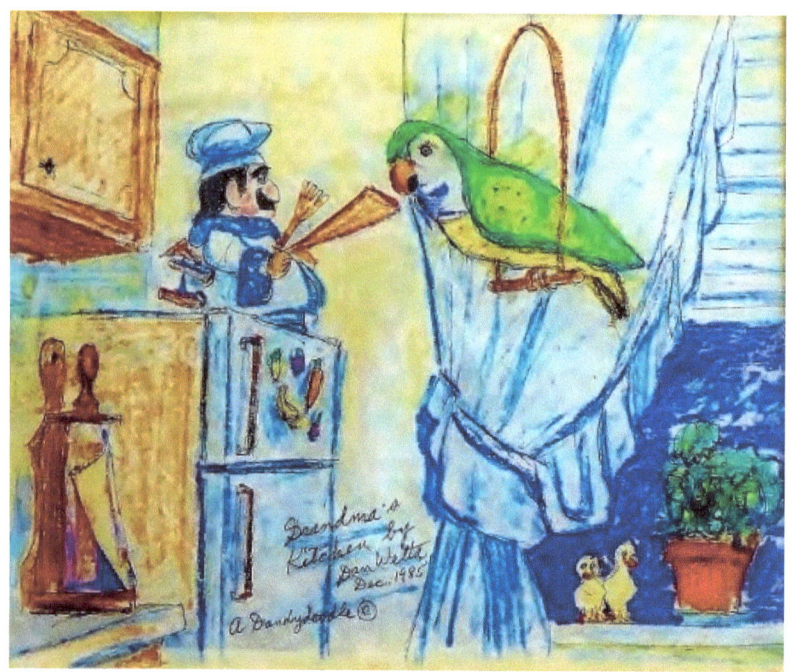

Title: Grandma's Kitchen
Size: 9 x 12 inches
Medium: Mixed media on paper
Copyright by Dan Wetta 1985

"Grandma" was my former wife's mother. Grandma was a genteel Southern lady, very proper, and she liked to cook. Unfortunately, her sister was married to "Coatwright," who was alcoholic. Whenever he was in the neighborhood, "Coatie" would stop off at Grandma's, and she would give him a quick glass of wine or sherry, and then she would hurry him on his way to get him out of her hair.

One time when Grandma was entertaining some neighbors, Coatie dropped in. Embarrassed, Grandma immediately took him to the kitchen for his glass of wine, because she knew he would leave as soon as he had had his drink. On his way out, however, he instead plopped himself down on the sofa with Grandma's guests in the living room. With slurred speech, he asked them if they knew who "hickeys" were.

When he only received puzzled looks as a response, he explained that the hickeys lived in communes in California! My sons, Daniel and Stephen, then teenagers at the time, fell off their chairs laughing. To them, hickeys were the passion marks left by kisses on the neck. It was a mistake of great amusement to confuse hippies with hickeys! Daniel and Stephen count that as one of the funniest family "Coatwright" stories.

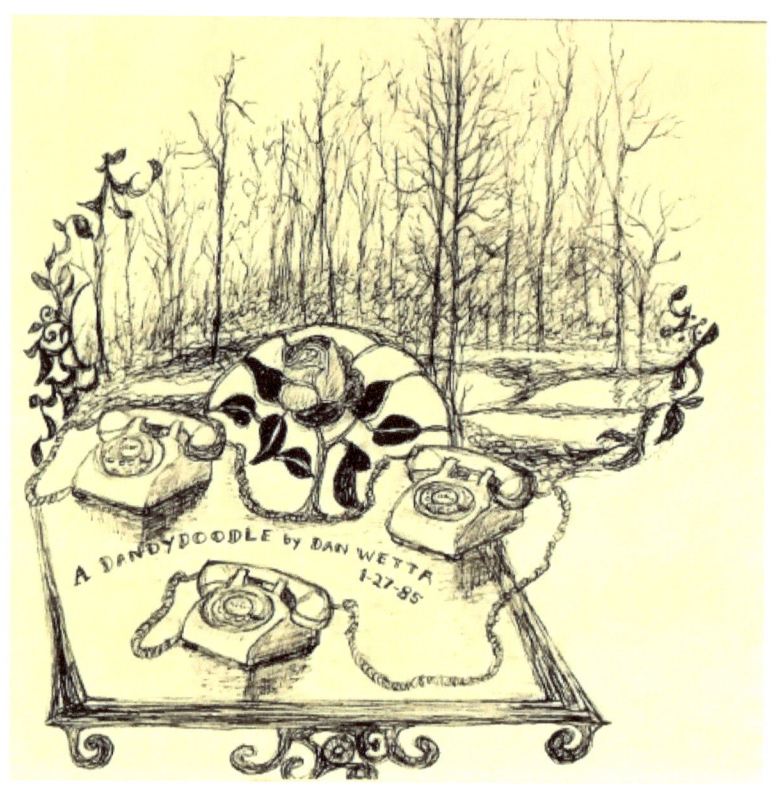

Title: Three Rotary Dial Phones
Copyright by Dan Wetta 1985

If you remember rotary dial phones, you're probably drawing a social security check every month!

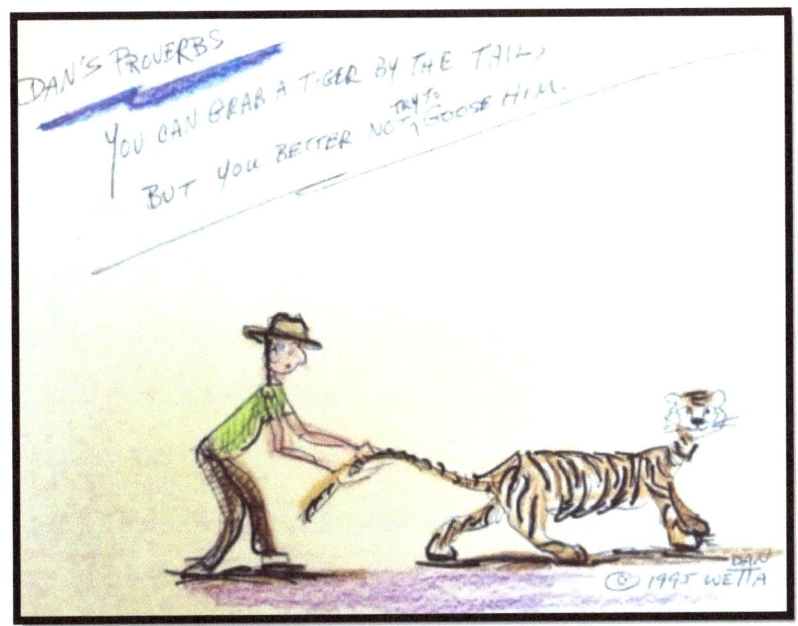

You can grab a tiger by the tail, but you better not goose him.

Title: Grab a Tiger
Copyright by Dan Wetta 1995

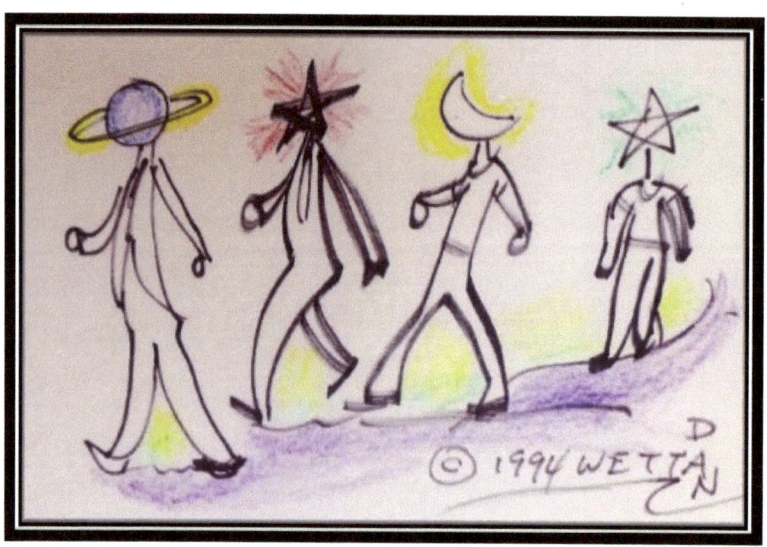

Title: Men from Outer Space
Copyright by Dan Wetta 1994

I think women from outer space will be visiting us soon also. I'm anxious to see what they look like.

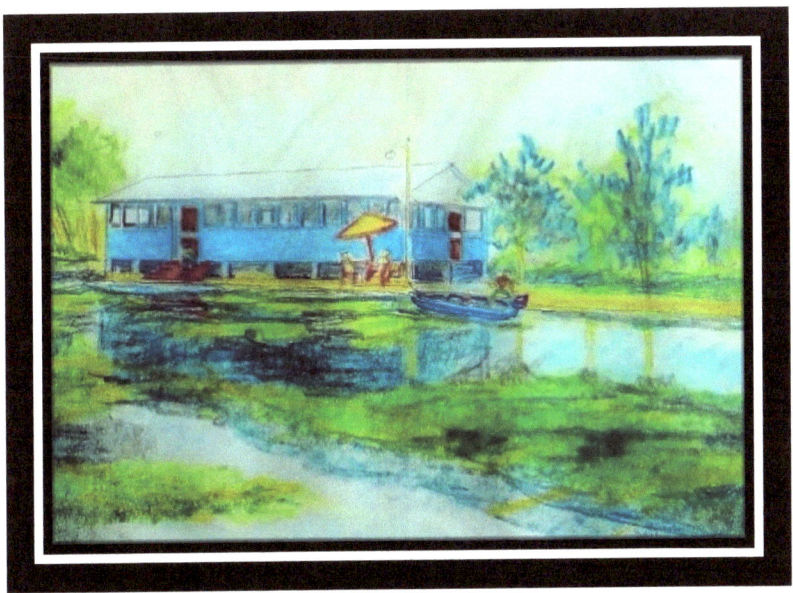

Title: Camp House in Louisiana Swamp
Size: 16x20 inches
Medium: Mixed Media on paper
Copyright by Dan Wetta

This place belongs to a friend of my brother JJ. Alligators are probably lurking in the water there.

When I was about four years old, my daddy brought me a baby alligator and placed it in a pan of water under the kitchen sink, where my mom washed the dishes.

The alligator began to grow, so Daddy got a metal wash tub for it. However, Mama was not very happy about that alligator under her kitchen sink!

The next day I heard Mama "raising Cain" with Daddy about the alligator under her kitchen sink, and the day after that, the alligator was gone. Mama won that one pretty quick.

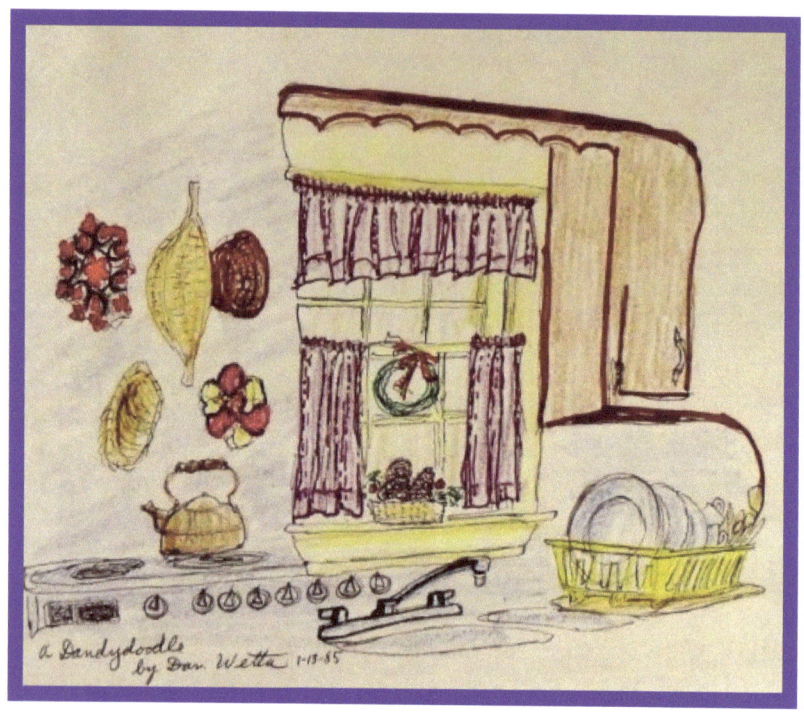

Title: Judy's Kitchen
Copyright by Dan Wetta 1985

This was my daughter-in-law's kitchen, but now it is my granddaughter April's kitchen. When I was visiting there in 1985, I looked out that window early in the morning and saw a little fawn in the back yard.

April was about eight or nine years old at the time. I woke her up and said, "Quick, come see the baby deer!" But it was gone. April went back to sleep.

Thirty years later, a strong wind gust blew down two trees onto the roof above the kitchen. It destroyed much of the house. April had bought this house that she grew up in from her parents: my son, Daniel, and daughter-in-law, Judy. The home was renovated in the same lot. April now has a renovated kitchen, but this window is still there.

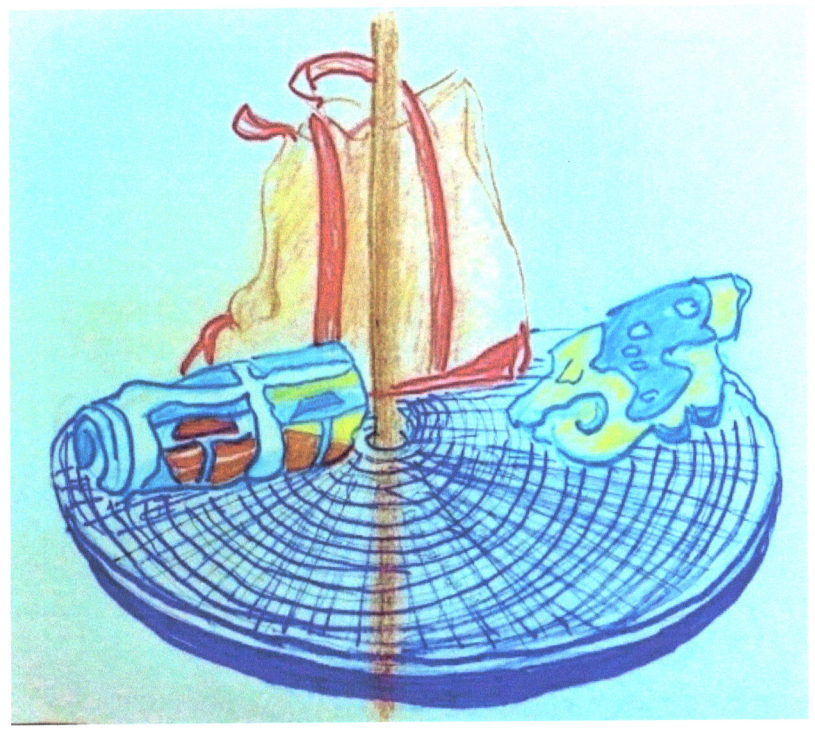

Title: A Can and What Else
Copyright by Dan Wetta

I do not know what this is, but a doodle is a doodle.

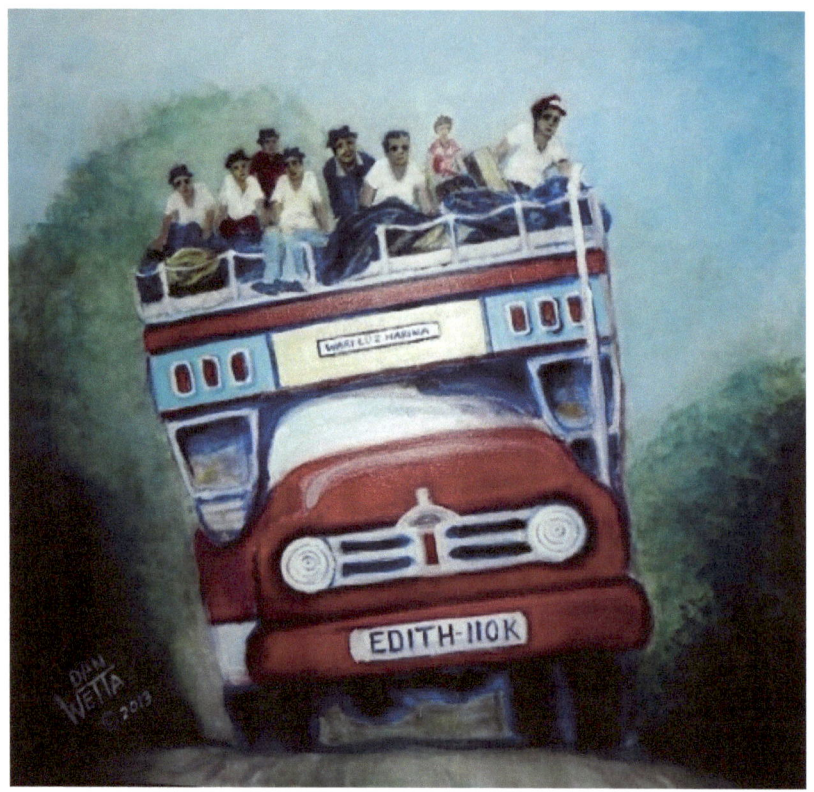

Title: Chiva Bus Colombia
Size: 36 x 36 inches
Medium: Acrylic on canvas
Copyright by Dan Wetta 2013

Two of my friends from Colombia, Edith and Luz Marina, used to talk about the "Chiva" buses in Colombia.

There is the Chiva party bus, which takes tourists and partygoers to night clubs, and then there is the bus that mountain people ride from their rural homes to town, where they can sell their farm produce. The top of the bus is designed to carry things, not people, but the passenger area is usually full, so some of the people have to ride atop the bus with their farm produce: chickens, piglets, goats and what-not.

I don't think Edith ever rode the bus, because she used to ride to town with her mother in a family pickup truck loaded with farm produce, which they would sell in town. However, Luz Marina said that she used to ride inside the bus when she was a little girl. Luz Marina is a descendent of the Wari Indians, so I printed "Wari Luz Marina" as the destination of the bus. I showed Edith's name and her apartment number on the license plate.

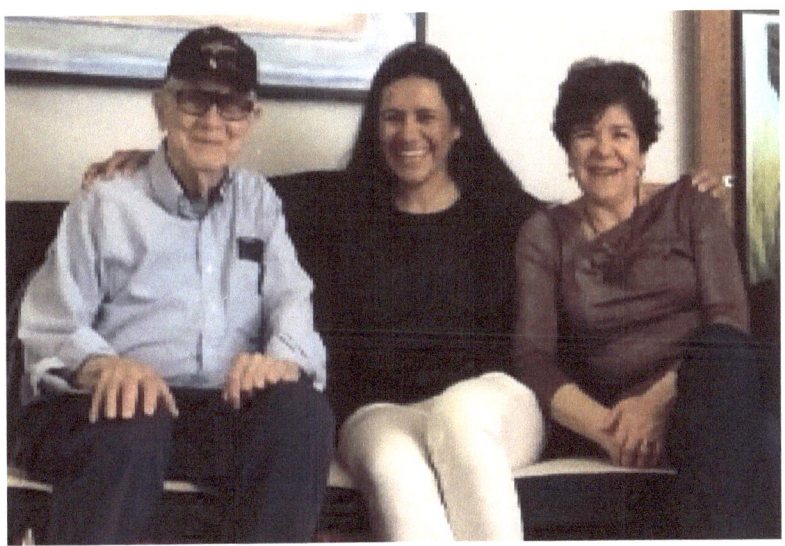

The Author, Luz Marina, and Edith

This is Luz Marina's recollection, as best as I could translate it from Spanish to English:

"When I was a little girl, I liked to travel in a Chiva bus. It was big and sturdy. I remember the smell of dried coffee, and it was very strong. We children did not have to pay a fare, but when the bus was full, we had to stand and hold onto the legs of our parents. I remember that in the middle of the Chiva in each aisle there was a pole that looked like a dance pole. I also remember that every time they hit a bump or put on the brakes, I hit my head or mouth on the pole. It tasted like iron.

"There are two seats near the driver on each aisle in the front of the bus. These seats are reserved for important or well-to-do people and for pretty girls. The drivers like to talk to pretty girls on the trip.

"However, nowadays people don't use the Chivas for transportation as much, because there are more comfortable buses available. The Chiva owner has decided to quit some passenger routes so that they can carry more sacks of dried coffee with protection from the rain.

"Also, they now use decorated Chivas as party buses that carry merry-makers from bar to bar."

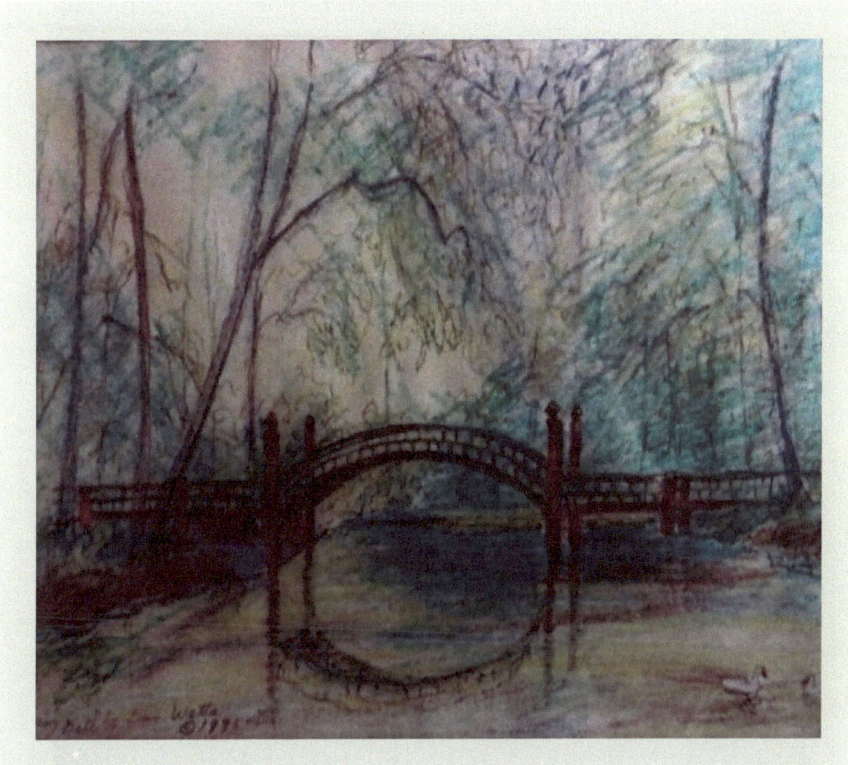

Title: Crim Dell
Size: 16x20 inches
Medium: Acrylic on canvas
Copyright by Dan Wetta 1995

This is my original sketch of Crim Dell on the campus of The College of William and Mary in Williamsburg, Virginia. Crim Dell has been photographed, drawn or painted thousands of times.

One day, when my son, Daniel, was a student at William and Mary, he was strolling around Crim Dell when he noticed a mama duck with her ducklings waddling along a sidewalk towards a sewer grating. Fearing that the ducklings would fall in, he tried to intercept the ducklings before they got to the grating. Mama duck misinterpreted his intentions and attacked him. Meanwhile, the ducklings did, indeed, tumble through the grating and into the cement run-off.

All turned out well however, because the opening was for rain water to drain off into the lake, and baby ducklings do swim very well!

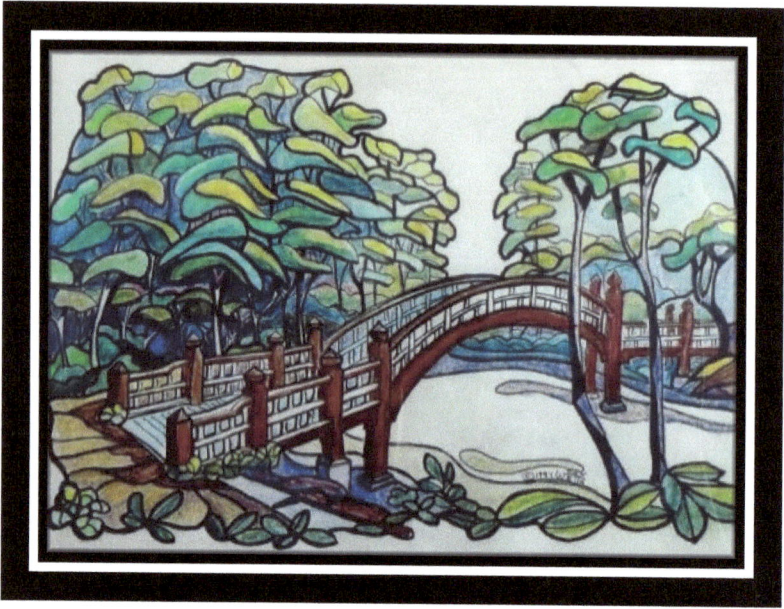

Title: Crim Dell Stylized one
Size: 12 x 15 inches
Medium: Acrylic on paper
Copyright by Dan Wetta 1997

Crim Dell has been painted and photographed by William and Mary students, photographers, and artists thousands of times. I did this stylized version of the bridge across the lake in a manner to set it off from those thousands of snapshots. Some others follow.

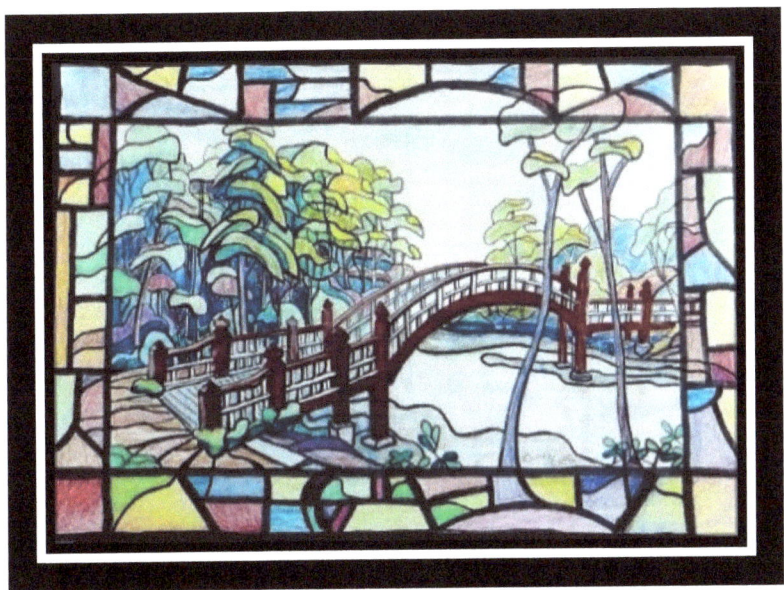

Title: Crim Dell Stylized 2
Size: 12 x 15 inches
Medium: Acrylic on paper
Copyright by Dan Wetta 1997

This is another stylized version of the bridge across Crim Dell. I wanted it to be different from the multitude of photographs that William and Mary College students have taken over the years. This one is in a painted "stained glass" pane.

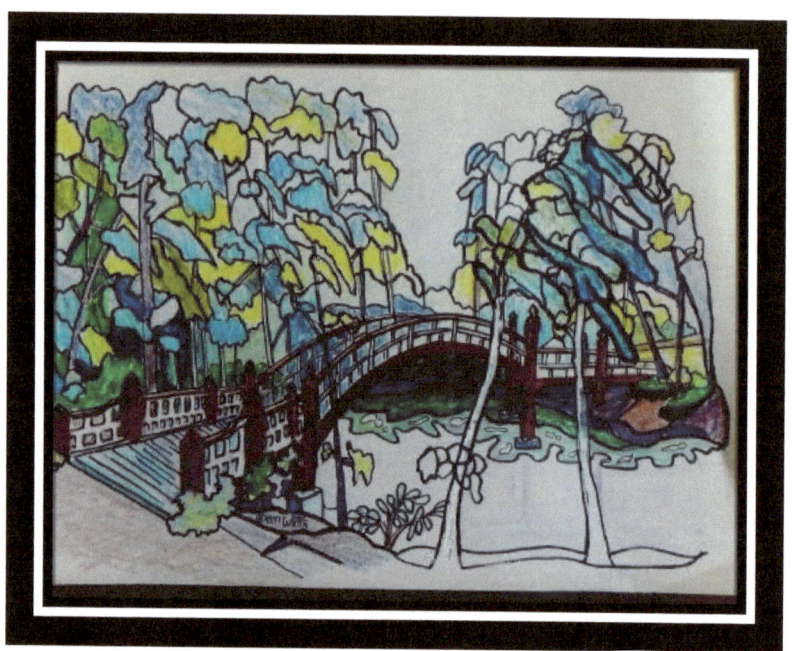

Title: Crim Dell Stylized 3
Size: 12 x 15 inches
Medium: Acrylic on paper
Copyright by Dan Wetta

This is the third stylized version I have done of the bridge over Crim Dell at the College of William and Mary. I painted it this way to set it apart from the many photographs that students have taken over the years.

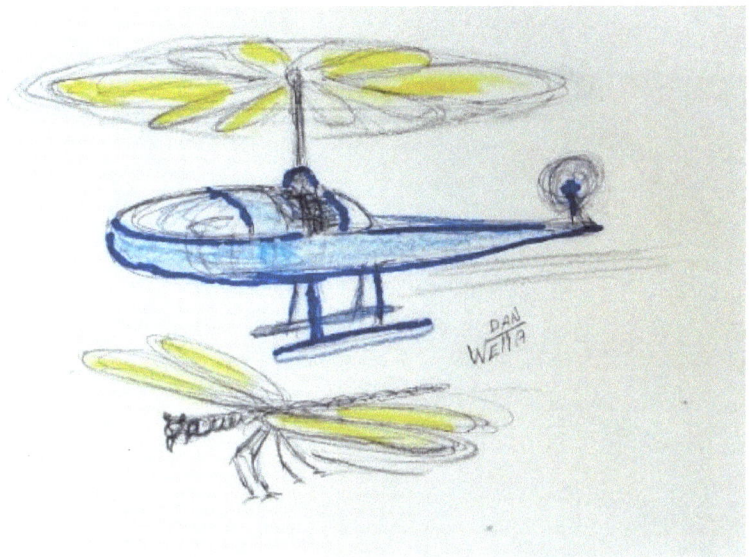

Title: Dragon Fly
Copyright by Dan Wetta

When I was a kid in Louisiana, we used to catch "Mosquito Hawks" and let them bite us, just to see how tough we were.

I suppose that there are lots of areas with so-called, "dragon flies," because their diet is flies. However in Louisiana, mosquitoes are everywhere.

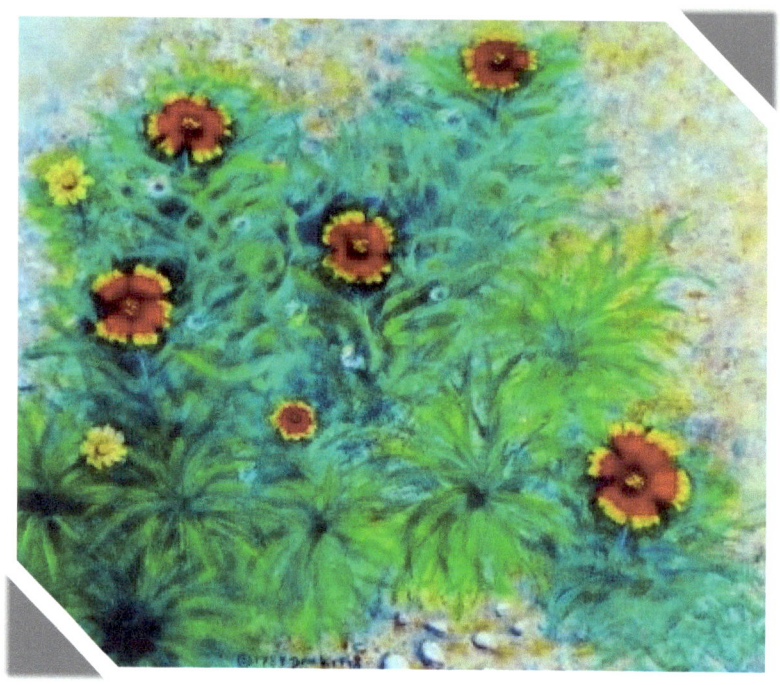

Title: Sand Flowers
Size: 14 x 16 inches
Medium: Acrylic on canvas
Copyright by Dan Wetta 1989

When my son, Daniel, had a condo on the Outer Banks of North Carolina, I was surprised to see wild flowers growing in the sand. I think these are called, "Fire Wheel" flowers.

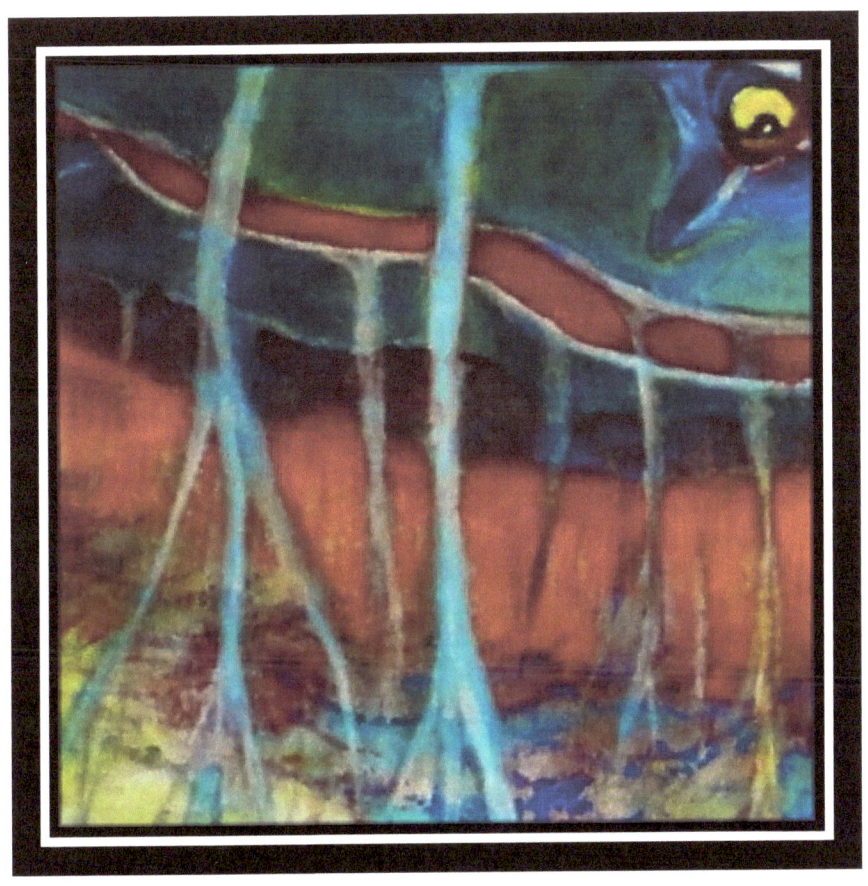

Title: Abstract: Quiet
Copyright by Dan Wetta 1989

This abstract was taken from my painting, "Quiet, Daddy's Meditating."

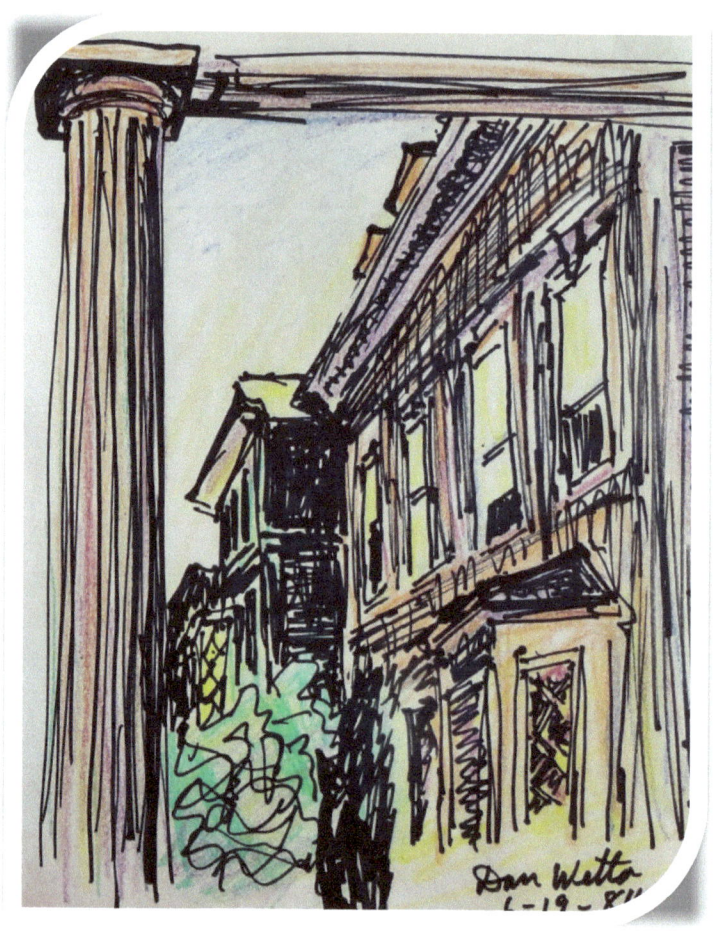

Title: Monument Avenue Apartment

When my son, Stephen, was going to Virginia Commonwealth University (VCU) in Richmond, Virginia, he used to live in an apartment on Monument Avenue, about two miles from VCU. Once in a while when I was visiting him, I would sit in the neutral ground on Monument Avenue and sketch the old houses there. However, you wouldn't want to linger around outside in the night time, because it was too close to a changing neighborhood on Grace Street in the VCU area.

On one occasion, Stephen was going to visit a friend on a side street off Grace Street, when he noticed a motorcycle thug approaching him. He ran up the steps onto the porch of a nearby duplex with the thug close on his heels. When he started down the steps of the adjacent duplex, a second thug was waiting for him and punched him in the gut. Stephen went down. They stole a few dollars out of his wallet and told him to keep out of their neighborhood.

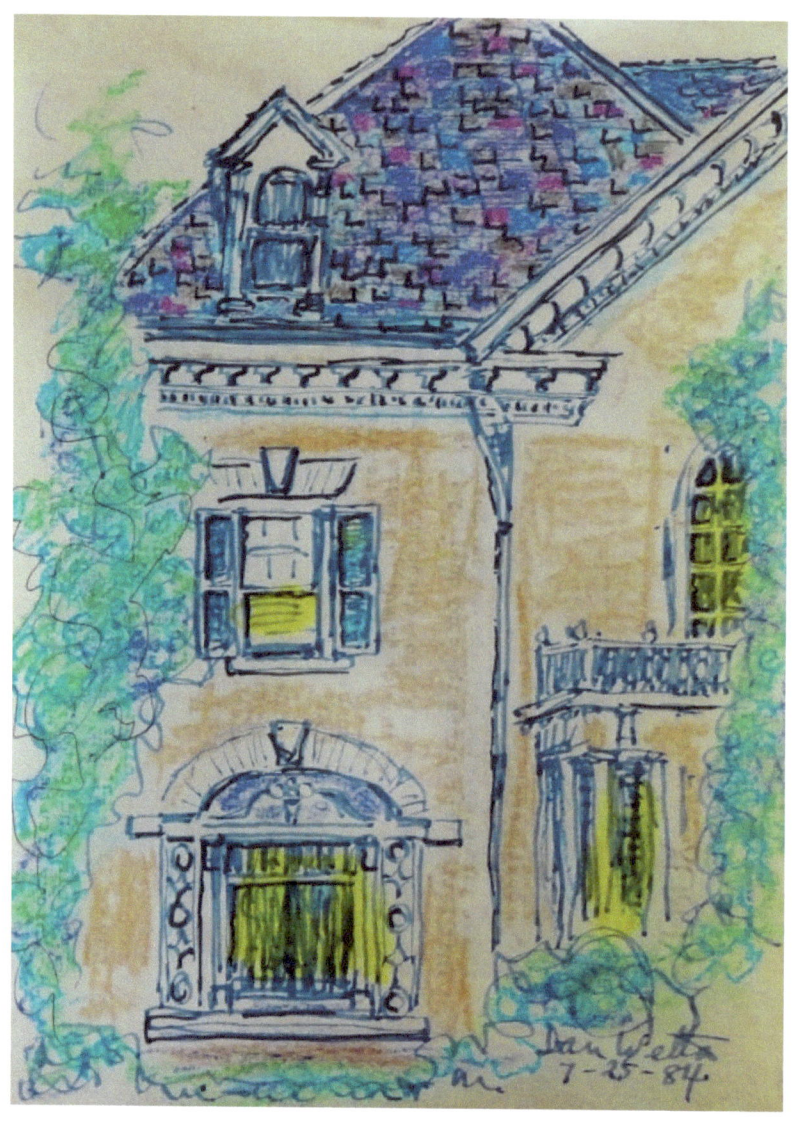

Title: Monument Avenue House

This is another sketch I did on Monument Avenue, and I will tell you about the time when my son, Stephen, got mugged and kidnapped in that changing neighborhood a couple miles away from here.

He went to pick up a girlfriend to go on a date, and when they came out of her apartment, an armed mugger was waiting for them. Stephen and his girlfriend gave him all the money they had, but the mugger threatened them with a pistol and said it wasn't enough. Stephen's girlfriend was street smart. She told the mugger that she could get more money from her brother, who owned a restaurant about a mile away on Grace Street.

The mugger agreed and ordered them into Stephen's car. The mugger got into the back seat with his pistol pointed at Stephen and told him to go to the restaurant. However, he apparently changed his mind and jumped out of the car and ran off when Stephen had to stop for a red light.

When the police came, one of them told Stephen that he couldn't believe that he and his girlfriend were still alive. When Stephen attended New York University a few years later, he said that he felt much safer in New York than he did in Richmond.

Chapter 6: "Mister D" Stories

"Mister D" was from Oklahoma. His name was Doris Persimons, and a kid from Oklahoma with a name like that had to fight all the way through high school.

And that he did. He was a semi-professional boxer for a while before he married Ms. Nana Mae, a well-to-do school teacher from New Orleans. They bought a house directly across from Mama's house on St. Andrew Street.

They had no children, so they took a liking to my three younger brothers. Mister D used to take them fishing in Lake Pontchartrain several times a month, and, at one time, Mr. D and his wife wanted to adopt my youngest brother, JJ, but of course, Mama would have none of that.

When we got married in Virginia, my wife, Martha, and I moved in with my Mama on St. Andrew Street and eventually rented an apartment in Mister D's back yard. It had a kitchen downstairs with a bedroom above. By this time, Martha was pregnant with our first child.

One night, we heard a clanging sound in the yard below, so we looked out the window to see what was going on. Rats had knocked the lid off a garbage can, and several of them were crawling all around. They were big as cats! Martha was terrified. All she had ever seen in Virginia were tiny field mice.

The next day she said wanted to go back to Virginia, where her mom could help her when her baby was born. And so we did.

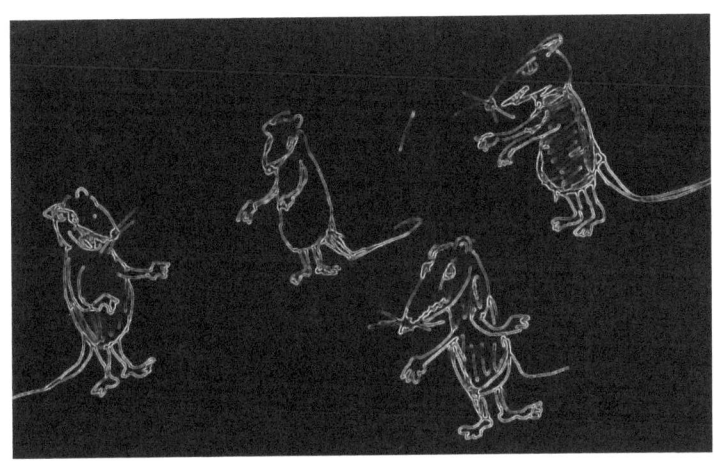

Mister D never had a job. Rather, he was an entrepreneur, and he would sometimes hire my younger brothers to help him. One time, when he was catering an event for the Jefferson Buzzards Carnival Club, he got into an argument with one of their members in the dining room, and before you knew it, he was in a fist fight with several Buzzards. He managed to hold them off while he backed up into the kitchen where my brother, Urban, was making sandwiches, and he slammed the door shut. He propped a chair against the door knob and yelled to Urban to jump out the kitchen window and run. Urban jumped out the window and started running up Magazine Street with Mister D close on his heels. They managed to escape, but they were afraid to go back for Mister D's car, so they walked over to St. Charles Avenue and went home on the street car. I do not remember what happened to his car.

One thing for sure, never start a fight with the Jefferson Buzzards!

Another time, he ran for a minor political office in New Orleans. I think it was called "Ward Captain." He placed a number of campaign signs in the neighborhood, and the next day, he saw some of his opponent's workers pulling up his signs. A fight broke out, and Mister D got arrested. That was the end of his political career.

There was a moving van company at the corner of St. Charles Avenue and St. Andrew Street, just a few yards away from Mister D's house. They started parking their tractor trailers in front of Mister D's house. Mister D didn't like that, so he paid my brothers fifty cents to let the air out of the truck tires. The manager of the moving van company saw my brother, Raymond, letting out the air out of the tires, and he came charging after him. Raymond ran under a house with the manager close on his heels, but the manager was too big to scramble very fast in such close quarters. When Raymond paused to look back at the manager from the other side of the house, the manager yelled out: "Now I got you!" Raymond replied: "You're over there, and I'm over here. You ain't got nobody!" Then Raymond ran up an alley, hopped over a fence and was gone.

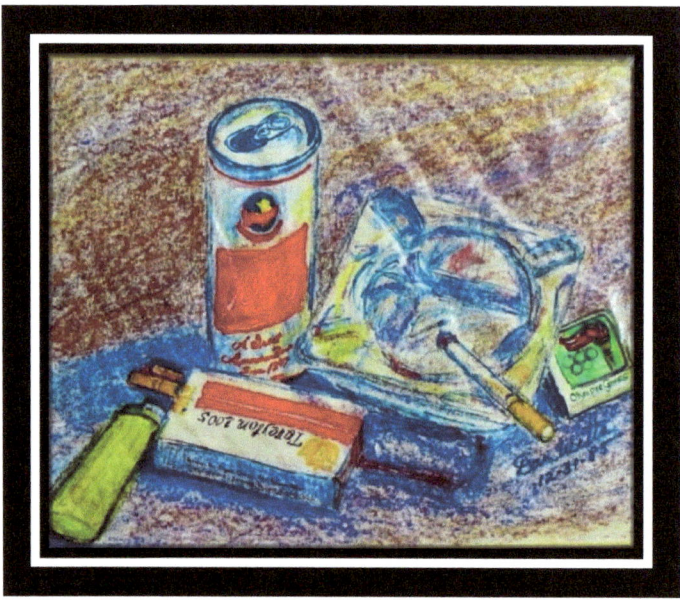

On another occasion, when Mister D was having a beer at a local bar, he accused a customer sitting next to him of snuffing a cigarette out in his beer. Of course, a fight broke out, and Mister D was banned from ever going back to that bar.

Yet again, Mister D took his car for repairs at a nearby gas station and accused them of ruining the motor in his car. The gas station owner denied it, of course, and refused to do anything about it. Mister D then persuaded my brothers, Raymond and JJ, to throw eggs at the service station. When the station was closed one evening, Raymond and JJ started egging it good, but the manager was still inside and came running out. Raymond and JJ took off. The manager was too fat to run, so he got in his car and almost caught them, but they ran the wrong way up a one-way street and got away, because the station manager didn't want to drive his car the wrong way.

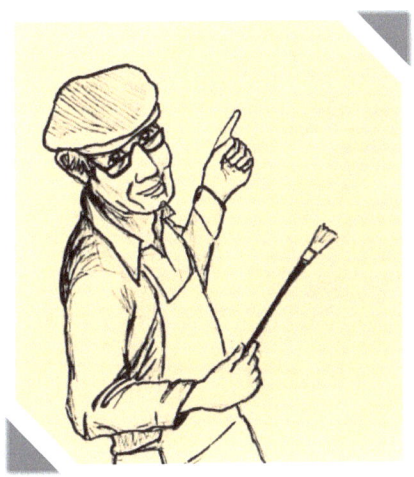

No kidding, all those Mister D stories are true.

Chapter 7: Dan's Grab Bag of Stories

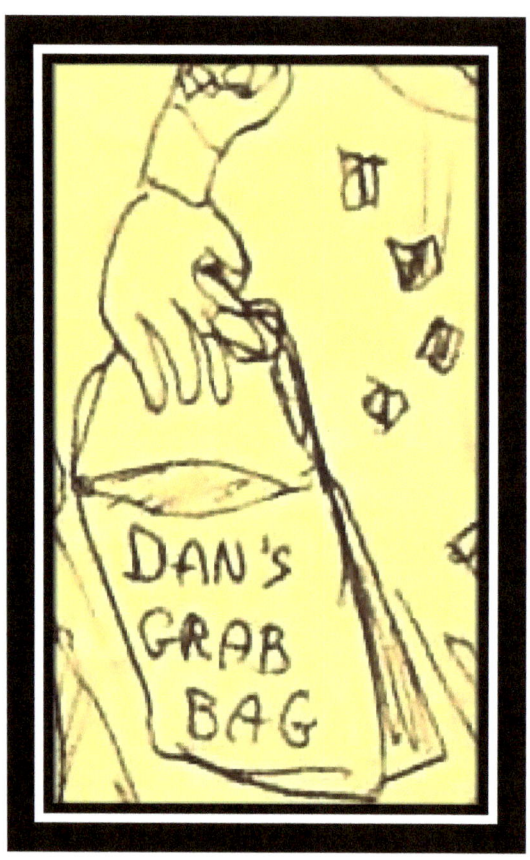

How many times have you heard people say: "I could write a book" They were thinking of all the funny (and sometimes sad) things that their children or grandchildren did. However, they never write the stories, but I am now going to start pulling memories out of my GRAB BAG randomly:

GRAB BAG:

I was never much of an athlete, certainly not a boxer. But a couple of tough brothers who lived across the street from us on Washington Avenue in New Orleans decided to teach me how to box. Floyd set up a boxing ring in our side yard, and we had boxing matches for the neighborhood kids. I guess I did OK, because there was an Irish gang that would bully me and my friend, Wilmer. So, after I had several boxing lessons, I stood up to their leader, Mike Ryan. I think he was surprised, because I was defending myself pretty good, until he pushed me into a big bush. He began pummeling me while I was tangled up in the bush. I was in a tight spot. But daddy's cousin, Leo, just happened to come walking by. He thought the whole gang was beating me up, so he yelled: "Shame on you all, get away from him!" and they ran off. They never bothered me after that.

Floyd's older brother was a bright young kid. When he was about twenty-one years old, he got a job as office manager of an importer on Tchopitoulas Street by the Mississippi River. They say he embezzled $18,000 and got caught and was sentenced to jail for five years.

GRAB BAG

My wife and I moved from Virginia to New Orleans when we were first married, and I got a job as office manager in the French Quarter for a small company manufacturing boxes for frozen foods. I think it was on Chartres Street. My office opened onto the street, so panhandlers with a hangover would come in during the day, asking for 25 or 50 cents. After a week or so, I got bright idea. When the next guy came in, I said: "If you want to make a few dollars, I think they need somebody to sweep the floor in the back. Let me ask the foreman." He began stammering and making excuses as he backed out the door. The same thing happened over and over again after that.

GRAB BAG:

Oh yeah, my youngest brother, JJ, was in the Redemptorist Grammar School band. One day he got together with a few other band members and they began playing Dixieland Jazz music. A nun grabbed JJ's clarinet and bopped him over the head with it. Mama got mad with the nun and made JJ stop taking music lessons.

GRAB BAG:

My brother Raymond did a little better. He played the clarinet in the Warren Easton High School Band with the famous Pete Fountain of New Orleans.

GRAB BAG:

When I was at the Seminary, I was no good at sports, except for track. I used to take first place in the mile-and-a-half mile runs in every track meet. Sometimes, I would come in fourth place in the quarter mile. A hot shot jock, Jake Mahoney, used to vie forr first place in the quarter-mile run with my buddy, Ivan. One day, I was running behind them in fourth place on the home stretch when Ivan began stumbling. As Jake tried to go around Ivan, I sped through an opening to take first place while they were stumbling all over the track. Jake was furious that a nerd like me could get the best of him. He left the seminary that year, and I heard that he eventually became a sports announcer.

GRAB BAG:

When the Catholic Church used to say Mass in Latin, my brother Raymond believed Latin was God's language, and that priests were special because they were the only ones who could talk with God. On the other hand, when I first started taking catechism lessons, I used to view priests as Sin Police who were always trying to catch you committing a sin.

GRAB BAG

Around 1931, a mad dog was roaming the streets of New Orleans. He bit several people, including my younger brother, Raymond, who was riding his tricycle on the sidewalk in front of our house. I was around the corner playing with a neighborhood kid when it happened. When I came home, my sister, Joan, was on the front porch waiting for me. She ran down to me and said:"Raymond got bit by a mad dog. Mama took him to the hospital to get rabies shots.

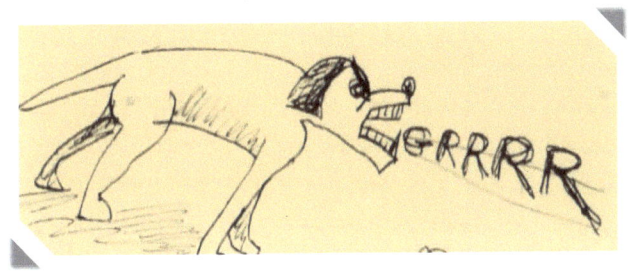

Title: Mad Dog Raymond

Raymond and I used to sleep in the same bed, but that night, mama had to put me in another bed, because I was terrified that Raymond was going to start foaming at the mouth in the middle of the night and start biting me.

GRAB BAG

One time, when my granddaughters were in high school, my son and daughter-in-law had to go out of town for a day. They said that the girls could take care of themselves, but maybe I could stop by to see how they were doing, so I went to their house, but nobody was home. I went to the kitchen for a glass of water, and sat down at the kitchen table. I happened to glance at the trash can which was full - full of empty wine and whiskey bottles!

I pulled each bottle out and lined them up on the kitchen table. About thirty minutes later, April and Keira came home. I didn't say a word when Keira appeared at the kitchen door and saw all the bottles on the kitchen table, but you should have seen the look on her face! She said: "It's not what you think, Grandpa. Some boys came by to see us, and they decided to clean out their car."

I accepted her explanation because if they had consumed that much alcohol, the house would have been a wreck, a total disaster, but it was in good shape.

GRAB BAG

When my great-granddaughter, Tawnie, was three or four years old, we took a walk around the lake near Dan Jr.'s house. Tawnie was walking Dan Jr.'s dog, Buddy. I saw some ducks on shore, and they seemed to be afraid of something in the water. I told Tawnie to hold Buddy's leash and stay where she was while I went closer to the water to investigate. After I had walked about twenty paces, Buddy pulled Tawnie down on her face when he suddenly made a dash for the ducks. When we got home, Tawnie told Granny: "Buddy pulled me down and didn't even apologize."

GRAB BAG.

After Mama died, my sister, Joan, took over as matriarch of the family. She arranged family outings, patched up disputes among family members, and also did charity work. On one of my visits to New Orleans, she told me she had ovarian cancer and that she was going to the hospital for a treatment the next day. I had a reservation to fly back to Virginia on the day of her treatment, so my brother, Urban, took me by the hospital on our way to the airport, so I could say goodbye to Joan. When we left the hospital, I told Urban: "The next time I come to New Orleans, it will be for Joan's funeral." But I was wrong. Joan had a strong will, and she survived for about ten or twelve more years. She continued to do her charity work. She was a volunteer at her Parish Food Bank, where she delivered food to needy people in the Parish. Her Parish would also pay their rent and utilities for the first few months or so, until they could get on the rolls of a Government Agency for more permanent aid.

Whenever I visited New Orleans, I would stay at Joan's house and sometimes help her deliver food staples to the needy. Usually, it would be a single mother with children who always, of course, lived on the second or third floor. I did a lot of huffing and puffing going up and down those stairs, but I was too much out of shape to blow the door down like a big bad wolf.

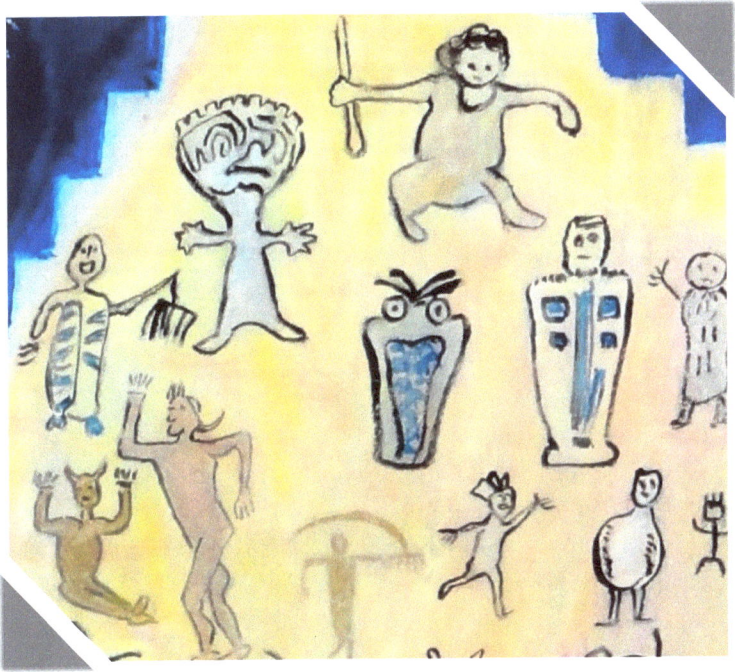

I could make an ancestry search and get statistics that tell me when my grandparents were born and when they died, but I would not know anything about their quirks, talents, faults, personalities or characters. So I am going to record what little I know of the personal lives of a few family members.

All I ever heard my dad say about his older uncles and cousins is that so-and-so died of pneumonia. My guess is that they died of the 1918 Spanish flu epidemic which killed over 40 million people worldwide.

My mom said that one of her uncles deserted the French army and immigrated to the United States, and my dad used to brag that one of his uncles was the first person to be killed by an electric street car. His uncle was carrying a bucket of beer when it happened. My mom asked daddy to stop telling that story.

My maternal grandmother used to live with Aunt Helen, mom's sister. Whenever we would visit Aunt Helen, she would tell me to be quiet, grandma Senac is upstairs sleeping. One time when we were visiting Aunt Helen, Grandma Senac walked slowly through the room where we were, and went upstairs without saying a word. It was if a ghost had just walked through the room.

In her old age, my dad's mother, Grandma Wetta, went to live with Aunt Mae, dad's sister. Whenever I would visit my cousin, Pete, Grandma Wetta would put us into double tubs in the shed and give us a bath. For lunch and supper, she would always open a can of green peas and carrots, which I could not stand. She used to say: "Eat all your peas and carrots. People in China are starving." I still do not understand how eating peas and carrots has anything to do with people who are starving on the other side of the world.

My dad lived with Grandma Wetta all the way into his late twenties. One time, he made a jug band base fiddle, using a bucket and a broomstick with a rope extending from the top of the broomstick to the bucket. He got a gig to play with a band in a barroom around the corner. Grandma Wetta found out, and went to the barroom, grabbed daddy by the ear, and dragged him home.

My dad's youngest brother, Uncle Richie, went to live with his sister, Aunt Bonnie, when he got out of the Navy. As far as I know, he was the closest anybody in our family came to being a hero. He was the bantam weight boxing champion of the Northern Fleet. He boxed in Russia. Uncle Richie had a heart attack when he was about 58 years old, and when I visited him at the Marine Hospital in New Orleans, he said to me: "I am down, but not out." But he was out. He died about a week later.

My sister, Anna Marie, says that Uncle Alvin's wife was stingy, because one time Uncle Alvin gave Anna Marie three quarters, but his wife said that was too much money for a little girl and took two of the quarters away from her.

Uncle Alvin was office manager of the United States Tropical Import Company during the 1930's, when Nazi Germany was on the rise. The US Tropical Import Company imported bananas, coffee, and other South American agricultural produce. I was about seven or eight years old when the United States established a Coordinator of Inter American Affairs (CIAA) to offset Nazi influence in South America, especially in Colombia.

Although I was only a kid at the time, I used to eavesdrop on conversations between my dad and family members, so this is my perception of what happened: Uncle Alvin discovered some sort of intrigue going on within the company, and he reported to his superiors that spies were operating within the company. Apparently somebody wanted to shut him up, so they said he was having a nervous breakdown. They had him committed to DePaul Sanitarium, a Catholic mental institution in New Orleans. Of course, the family was upset, and a week or so later, I overheard my dad and his brothers plotting to help Uncle Alvin escape from the sanitarium! However, they never followed through with the scheme.

Uncle Alvin was eventually released, but from that time on, he was a broken man.

One more story about Uncle Alvin:

My dad and Uncle Alvin continued to live with Grandma Wetta into their late twenties.

Uncle Alvin was coming home from a date late one night. He came through the back yard and attempted to open the back door. Daddy thought someone was trying to break in and took a shot at Uncle Alvin.

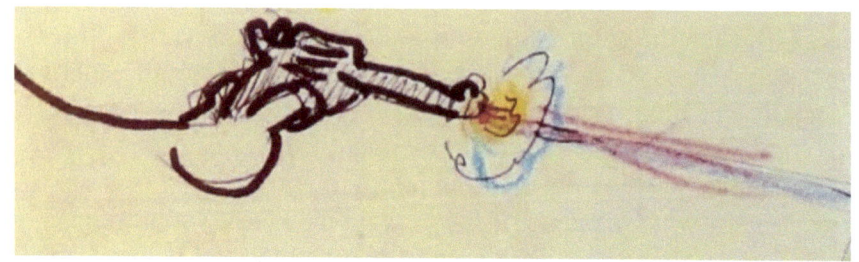

BANG! ...Uncle Alvin yelled out, "Joe!"

It's a good thing my daddy was a bad shot. Daddy was so upset that he got rid of his pistol and never owned one after that. Neither did I.

Chapter 8: Lions and Tigers

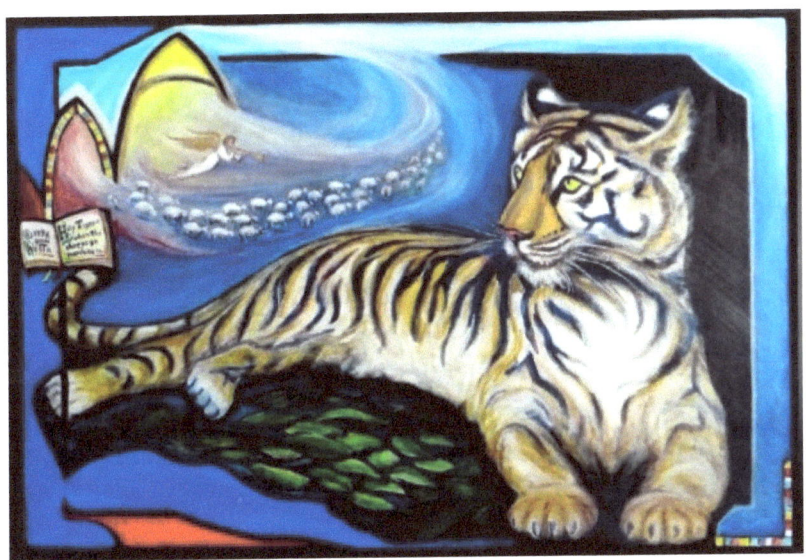

Title: Holy Tiger
Size: 24x36 inches
Medium Acrylic on canvas
Copyright by Dan Wetta 1996

I was playing Louis Armstrong's rendition of "When the Saints Go Marching In," when I was inspired to paint this tiger and flock of sheep.

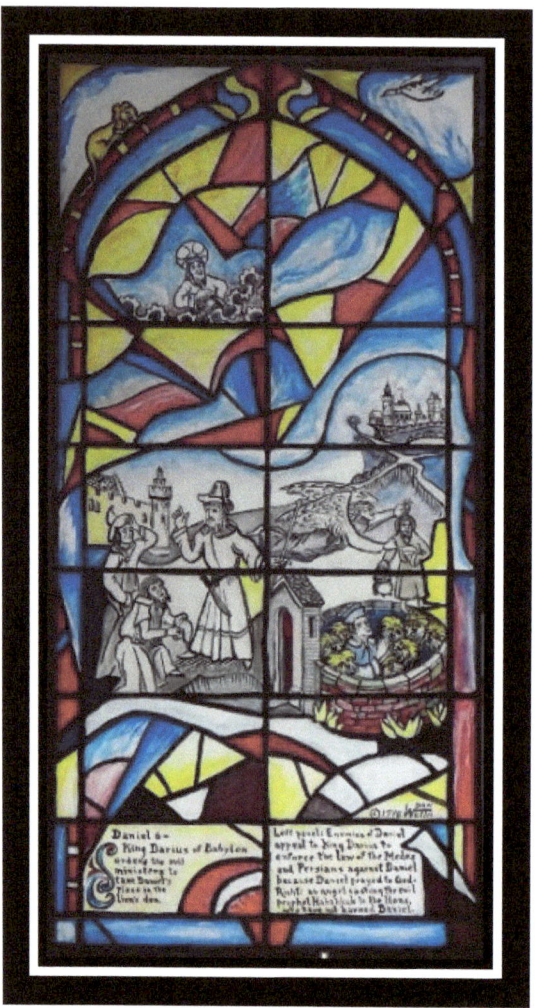

Title: Daniel in Lion's Den
Size: 18x36 inches
Medium Acrylic on canvas
Copyright by Dan Wetta 1998

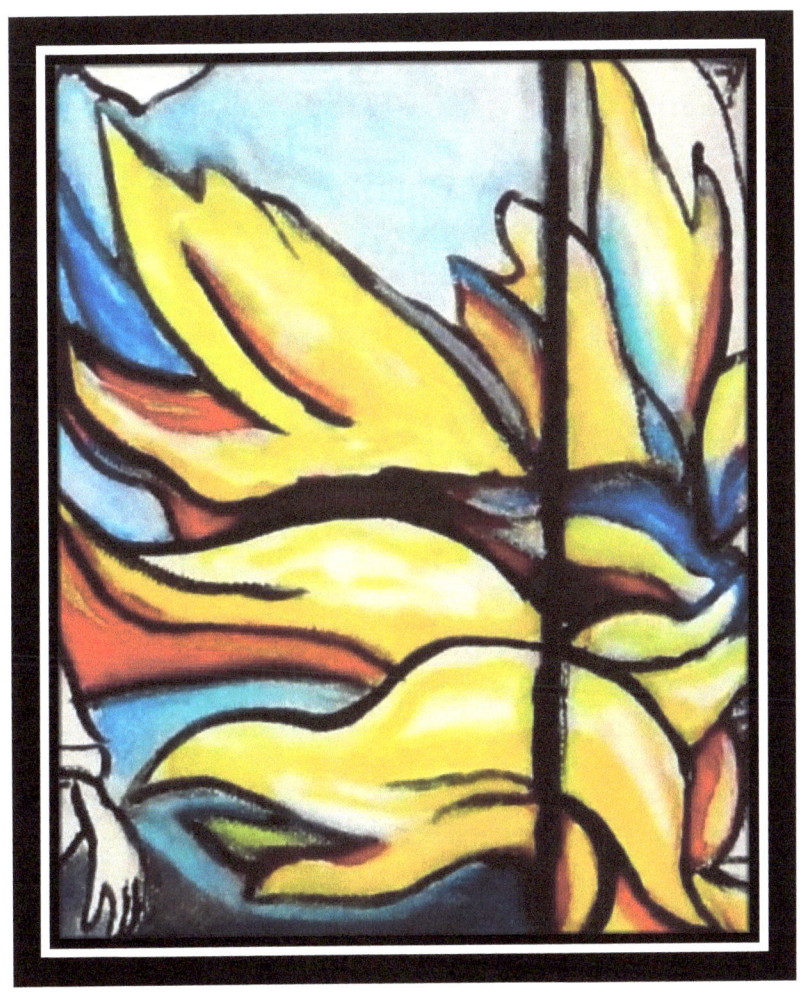

Abstract Thirty Eight
Copyright by Dan Wetta 1998

This is from my painting, "Fiery Furnace."

2 Kgs 17:24-28

The king of Assyria brought people from Babylon, Cuthah, Avva, Hamath and Sepharvaim and settled them in the towns of Samaria to replace the Israelites. They took over Samaria and lived in its towns. When they first lived there, they did not worship the Lord; so he sent lions among them and they killed some of the people. It was reported to the king of Assyria: "The people you deported and resettled in the towns of Samaria do not know what the god of that country requires. He has sent lions among them, which are killing them off because the people do not know what he requires."

Then the king of Assyria gave this order: "Have one of the Israelite priests you took captive from Samaria go back there and teach the people what the god of the land requires."

Title: Dinner Is Served (text)
"He has sent lions among them…"

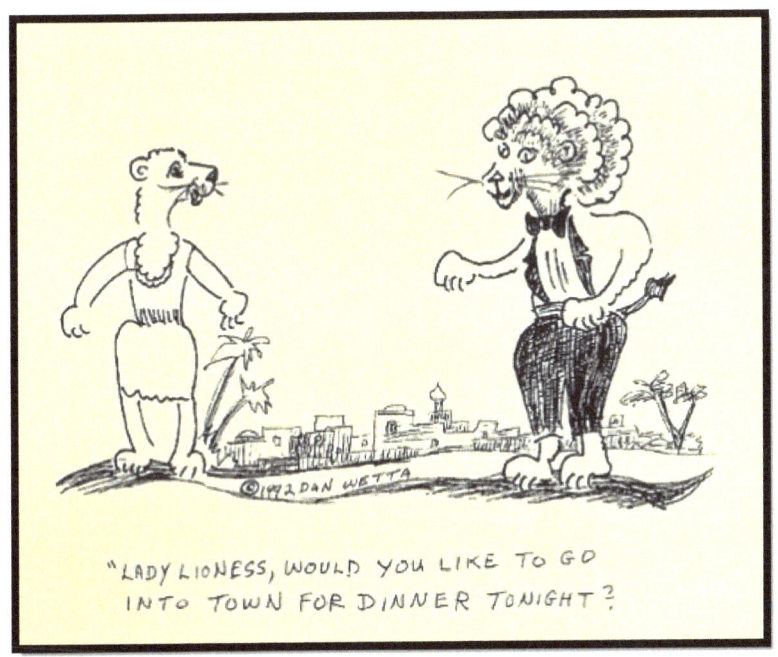

"Lady Lioness, would you like to go into town for dinner tonight?"

"Lady Lioness, would you like to go into town for dinner tonight?"

Title: cartoon Dinner is Served
Copyright by Dan Wetta 1992

See text for 2 Kings 17:24-28 (previous page).

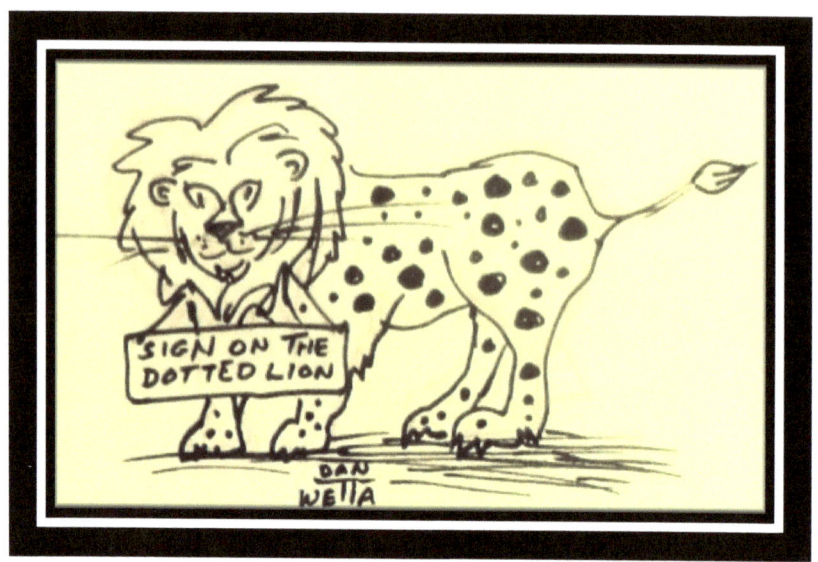

Title: Sign on Dotted Lion
Copyright by Dan Wetta

Well, if you don't think this cartoon is funny, you don't have to sign on the dotted lion.

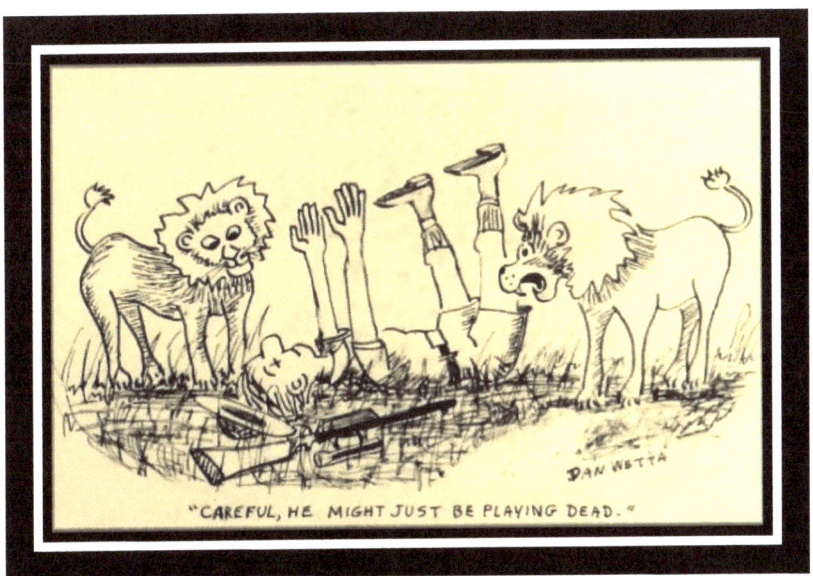

"CAREFUL, HE MIGHT JUST BE PLAYING DEAD."

Title: Careful
Copyright Dan Wetta

"Careful, he might just be playing dead." This is a reverse gag. Sometimes they are funny, sometimes not so funny. Another example of a reverse gag is: "Man bites dog."

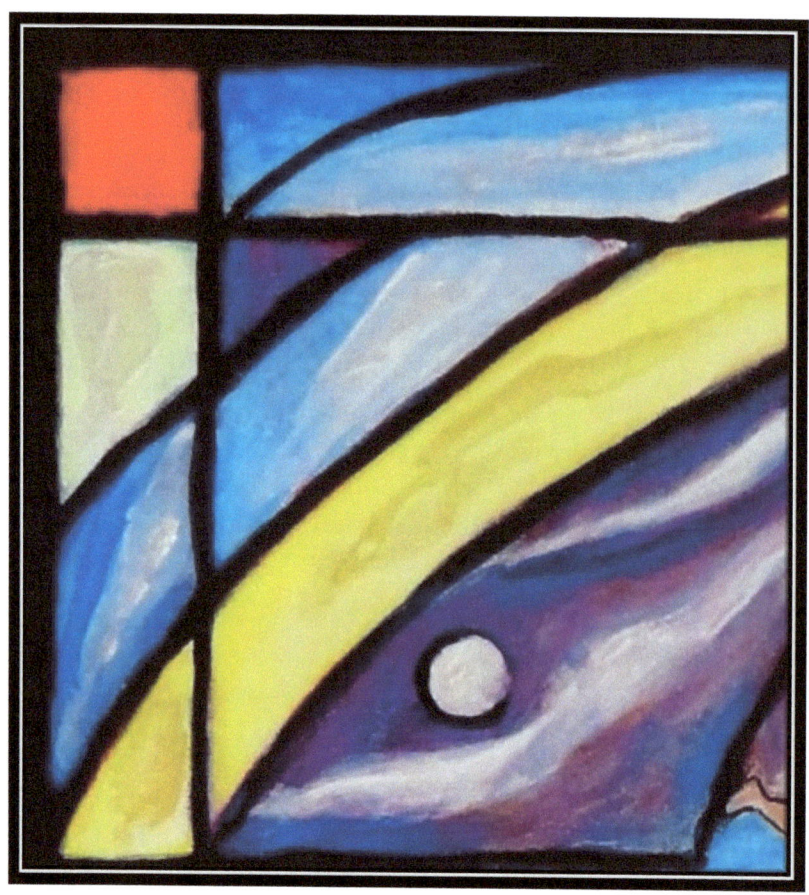

Title: Abstract Fifteen
Copyright by Dan Wetta 1997

This was cropped from my painting entitled, "Resurrection Lightning Bolt."

Chapter 9: Boats

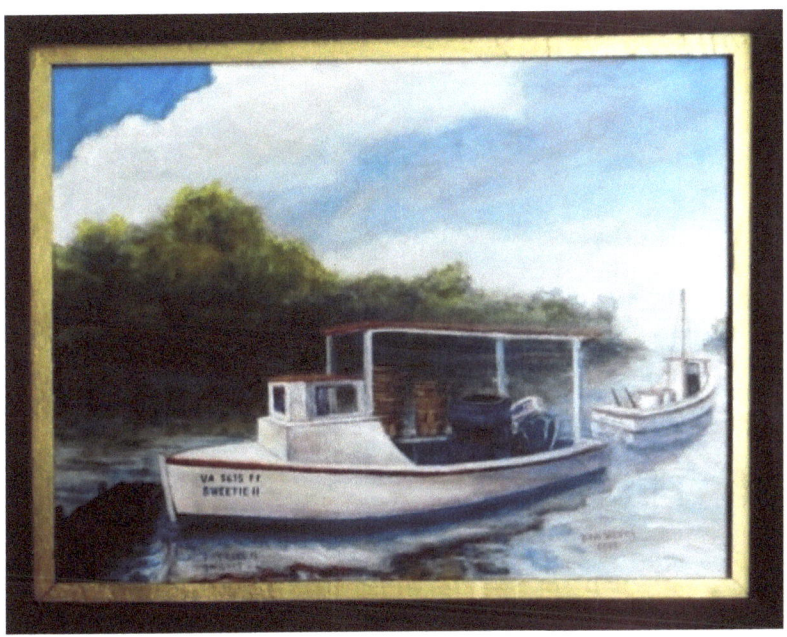

Title: Sweetie II
Size: 18x24 inches
Medium: Acrylic on canvas
Copyright by Dan Wetta 1984

I was driving, and I was lost when I saw "Sweetie II." I stopped and took a couple of snapshots and then started driving again. I eventually found my way home.

When I began painting Sweetie II, I noticed that the name of the boat in the background was Goat Island, so I googled Goat Island and found out that it is in King George County, Virginia.

Always nice to know where you are.

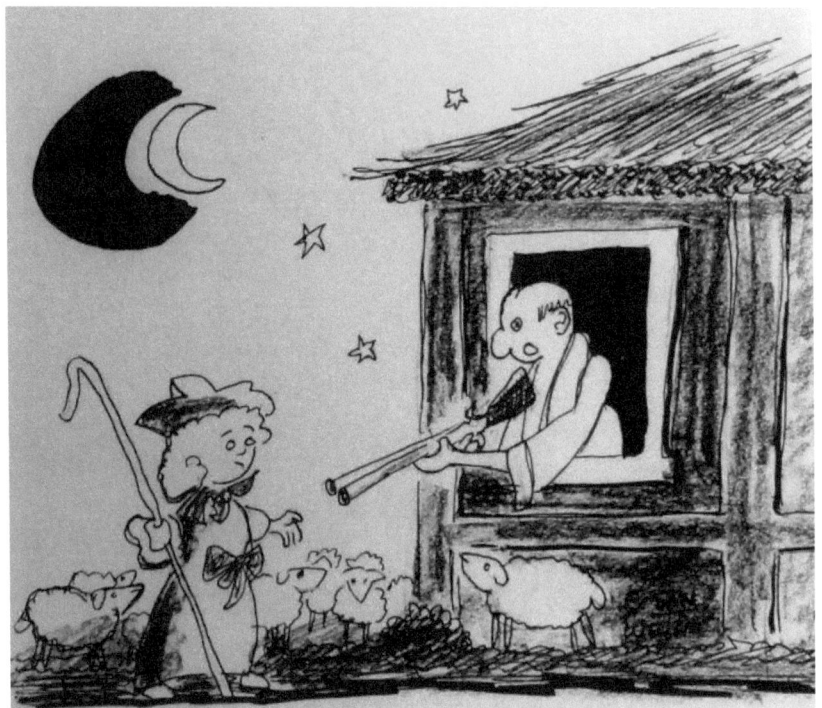

Go away! I do not want to count your sheep!

Title: Go Away

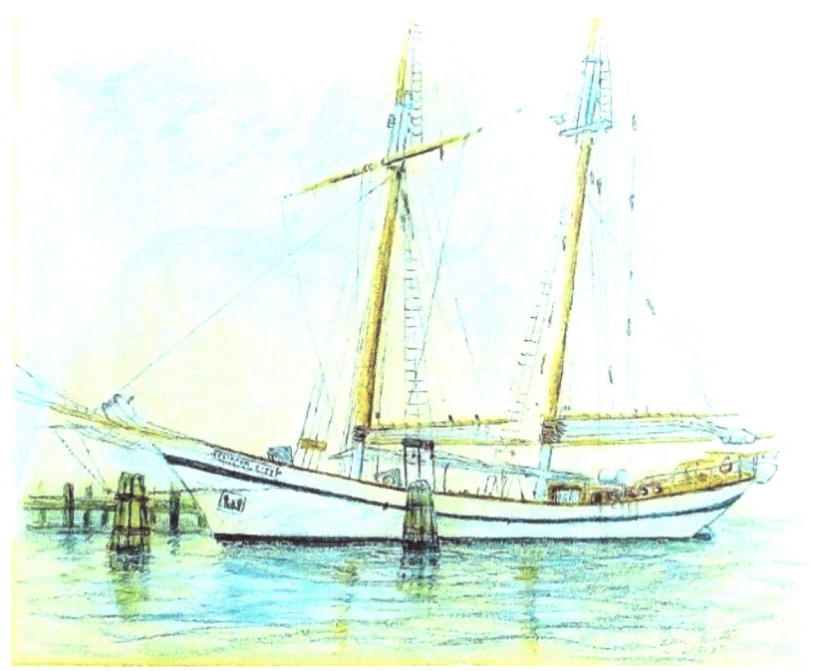

Title: Clipper City with Silhouette
Size: 12 x 16 inches
Medium: Mixed media on paper
Copyright by Dan Wetta 1987

When I took a photo of this tall ship, Clipper City, to sketch, somehow, I got my silhouette in the background. Look closely, and you will see me looming in the sky behind the ship.

Then, when I took another photograph of it to eliminate the silhouette, I put a lightning strike in the photograph, so I decided to include both images in my book.

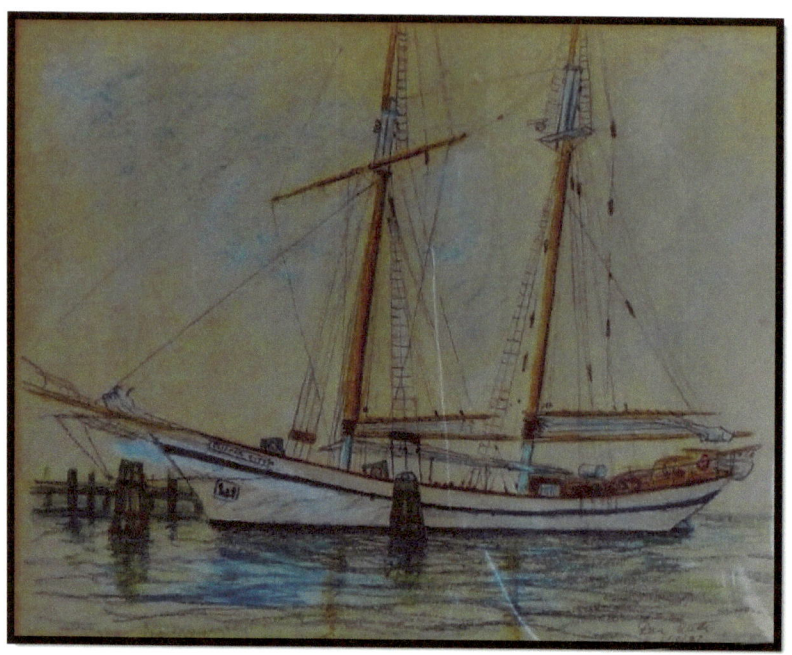

Title: Tall Ship with Lightning Strike
Size: 11 x 14 inches
Medium: Mixed media on paper
Copyright by Dan Wetta 1987

I am a lousy photographer. I was about to delete the snapshot I took for this sketch because of the white streak flaw, but I realized that it looked like a lightning strike coming down the mast, so I left it as it was. I think my ineptitude as a photographer paid off in this case.

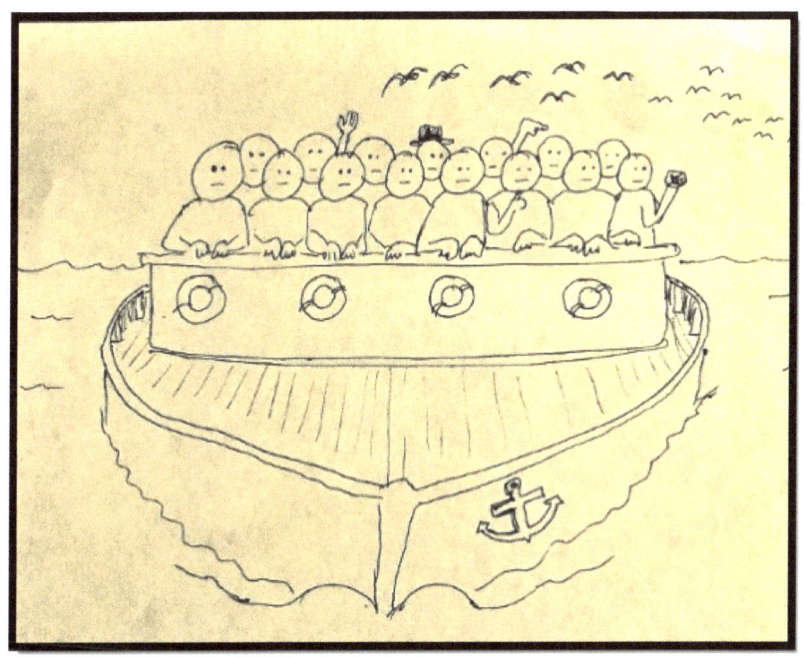

Title: Boatload of Lost Coins (Dud)
Copyright by Dan Wetta

I classify this cartoon as a "dud," but my son, Daniel, found it amusing. He called it a "shipload of money."

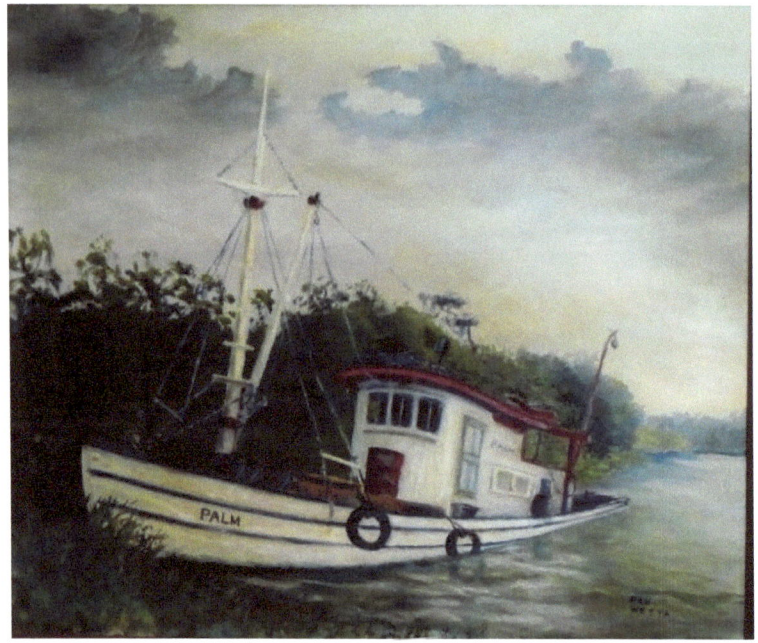

Title: Palm on the Bayou
Size: 20x24 inches
Medium: Oil on canvas board
Copyright by Dan Wetta 1968

This is one of a few oil paintings I ever did. I switched to acrylics around 1969.

My brother, Raymond, was driving me around the bayou country in Louisiana, when I spotted this half-sunken old shrimp boat.

"Stop the car," I said. It had been drizzling off and on all morning, and about a half hour after I had been drawing, it began to rain. We hustled back to the car and ate some sandwiches that my sister-in-law, Ann, had prepared for us.

It kept on raining, so my brother said, "Let's get a beer." We found a barroom on the bayou. I think it was Bayou Baritaria. Some customers at the bar were speaking Cajun French, which I didn't understand. I had studied French at St. Joseph's Seminary but did not keep up with it. Cajun French is a whole other thing, anyway.

After one beer it stopped raining, so we went back to the boat, and I finished my sketch.

Afterwards, we went back to Raymond's house in New Orleans, where Ann had a bowl of red beans and rice ready for us.

Chapter 10: Cows

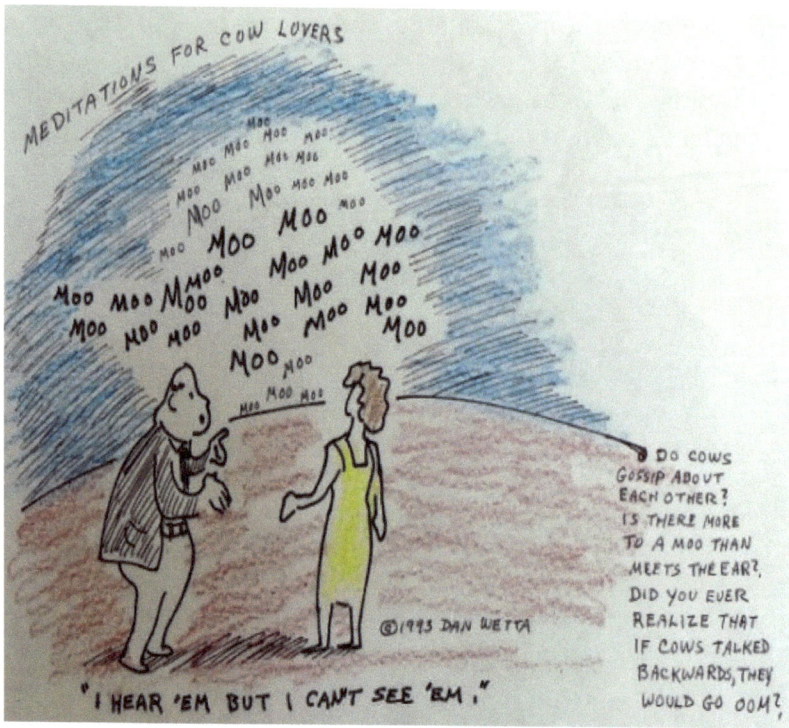

Title: We All Want to Moo Like a Cow

Why is it that whenever you are driving with your kids in the car, and you see a cow, you automatically moo like a cow? Everybody does this, so I am posting some meditations for cow lovers:

Do cows gossip about each other?

Is there more to a moo than meets the ear?

Do you realize that if cows talked backwards, they would go "oom?"

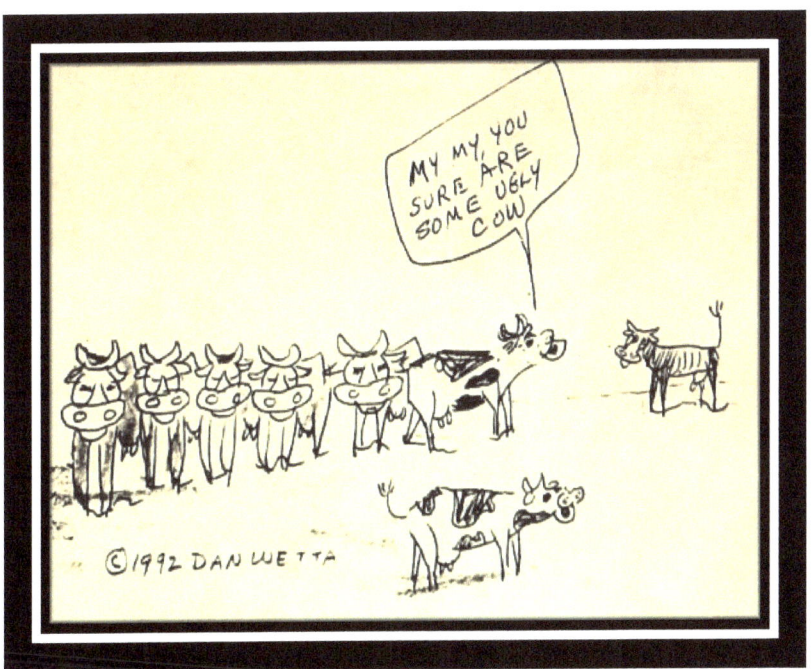

"My, my, you sure are some ugly cow!"

Title: Ugly Cow
Copyright by Dan Wetta 1992

You never know what cows are thinking!

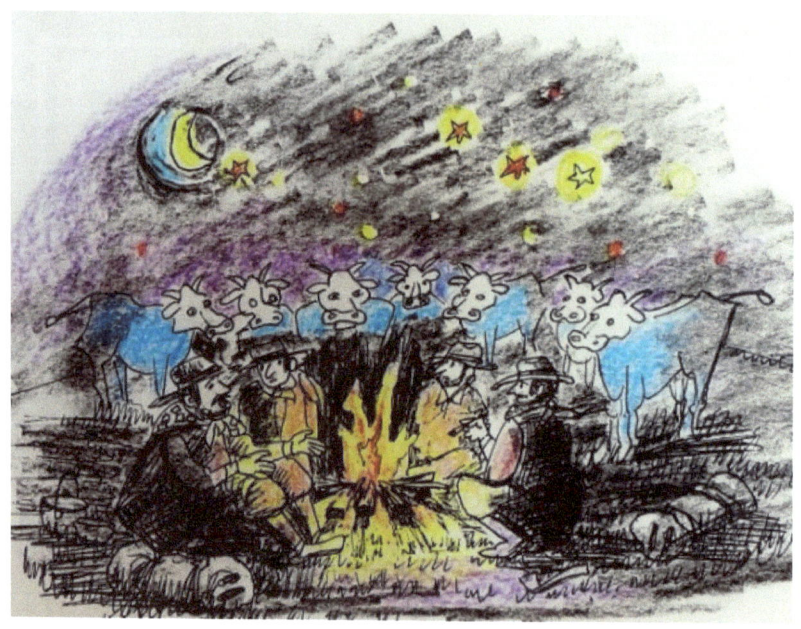

Title: Many Moos Ago
Copyright by Dan Wetta

It all happened many moos ago…

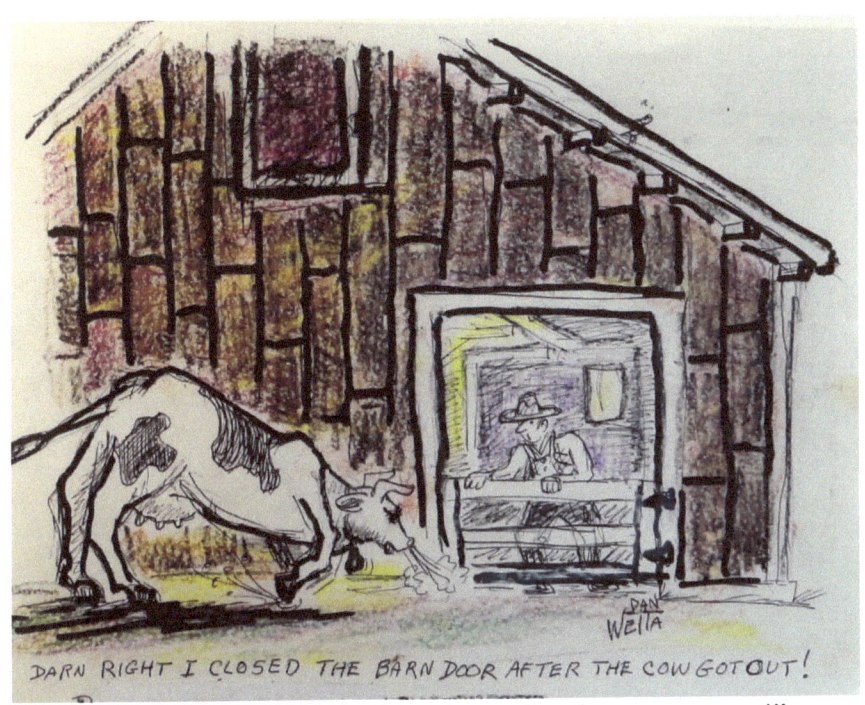

"Darn right, I closed the barn door after the cow got out!"

Title: Close the Barn Door
Media: Crayon and Markers
Copyright by Dan Wetta

Things like this happen all the time, but the Cow Milker's Association has been covering it up!

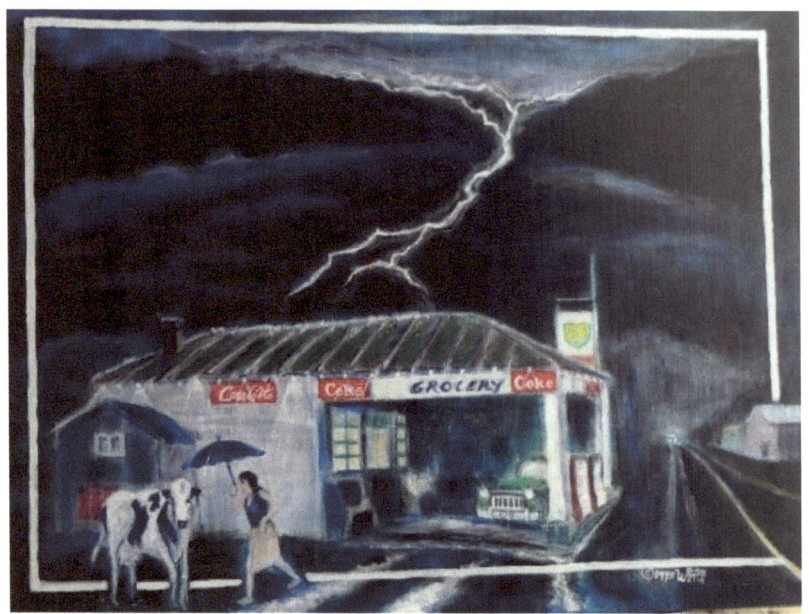

Title: Oh, The Cow
Size: 18x24 inches
Medium: Acrylic on canvas
Copyright by Dan Wetta 1995

I used to live within a mile of this country store and gas station on West Broad Street in Henrico County, Virginia. It was near Short Pump, Virginia, but it is probably gone by now.

On my way to work one bright, sunny morning, I pulled over to the side of the road and took a few reference snapshots of the store. I painted it a few months later. My original painting was a daylight scene. That just didn't seem right, so I turned it into a night scene and added a thunderstorm and a stray cow.

You know what happened after I did that?

A woman pulled up to the gas pumps during the rainstorm, and she saw the cow getting soaked in the rain. She exclaimed: "Oh, the cow!" She jumped out of her car and ran to the aid of the cow with her umbrella!

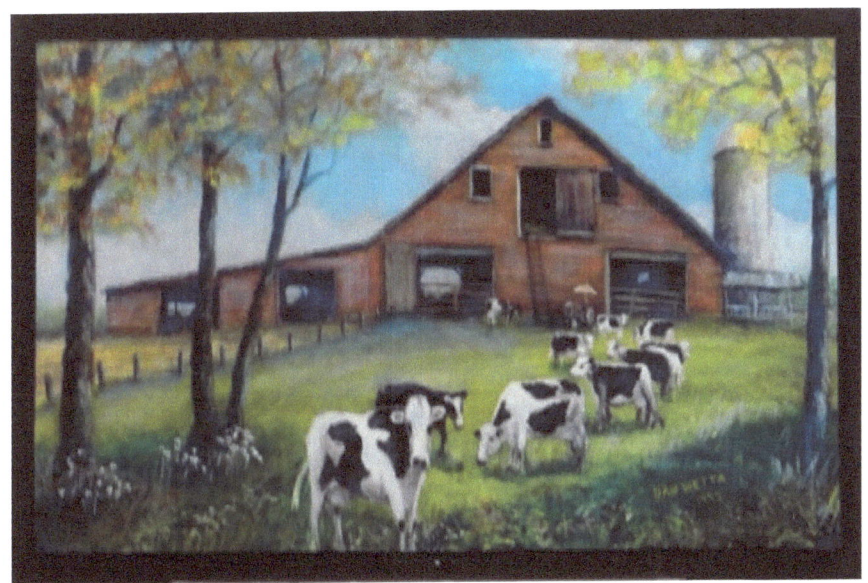

Title: Red Barn and Cows
Size: 18x32 inches
Medium: Acrylic on canvas
Copyright by Dan Wetta 1993

In my painting, Red Barn and Cows, do you see the optical illusion? It depends upon whether your mind thinks that you are looking straight-on at the barn, or if you are looking at it from a little to the side of it!

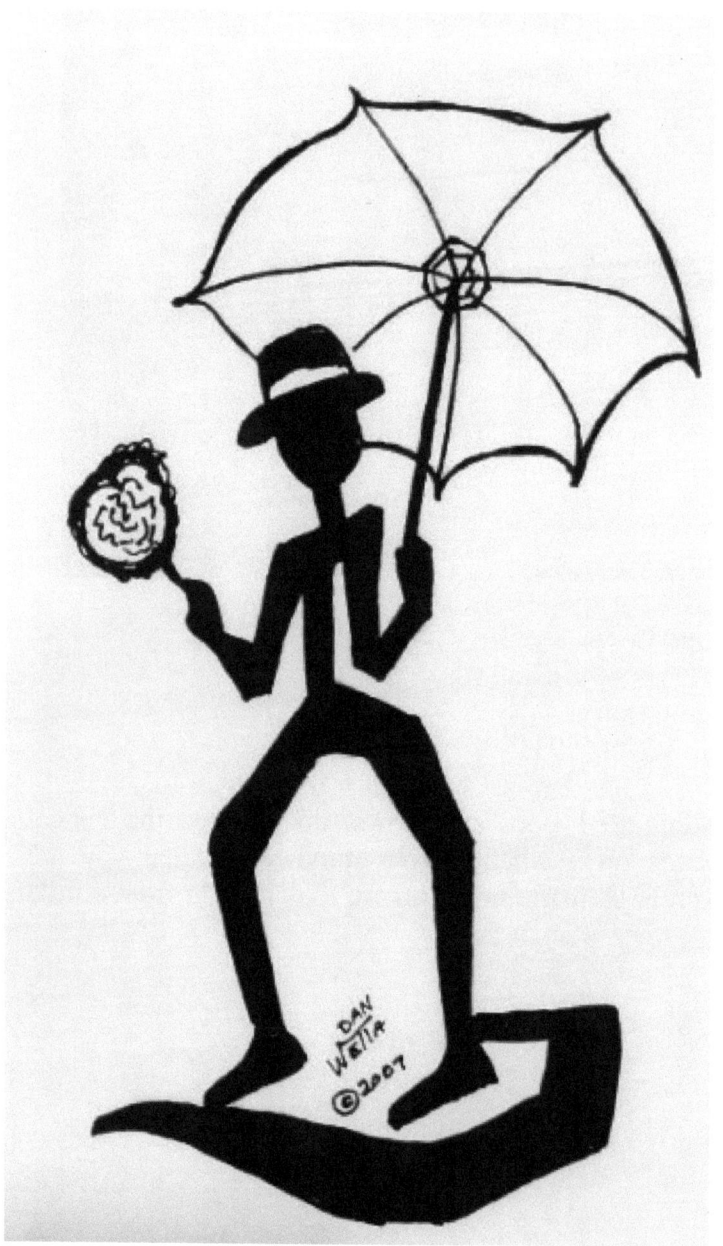

Title: Umbrella Man (Number One)
Copyright by Dan Wetta 2009

I did several of these Umbrella Man silhouettes for my niece, Nancy, who was going to copy and transfer the silhouettes onto T-shirts and sell them during the Mardi-gras season in New Orleans. Unfortunately, her business partner for this died, and so she never went through with it.

When God created light, He created shadow, which is the opposite of light. God created a lot of opposites. When He created light, He also, perhaps, created the maximum speed: the speed of light. Light travels at 186,000 miles per second.

No evolution was involved in the creation of light, speed and sound; rather, they were created instantly.

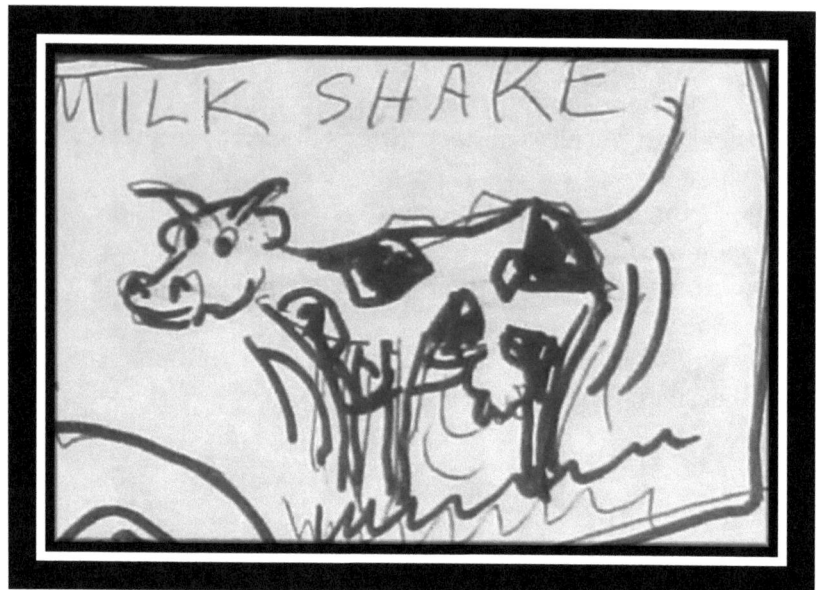

Title: Milk Shake
Copyright by Dan Wetta

There are only two kinds of cows:

Lucky Cows = Milk Cows (but they can get the shakes.)
Unlucky Cows = Hamburger Cows

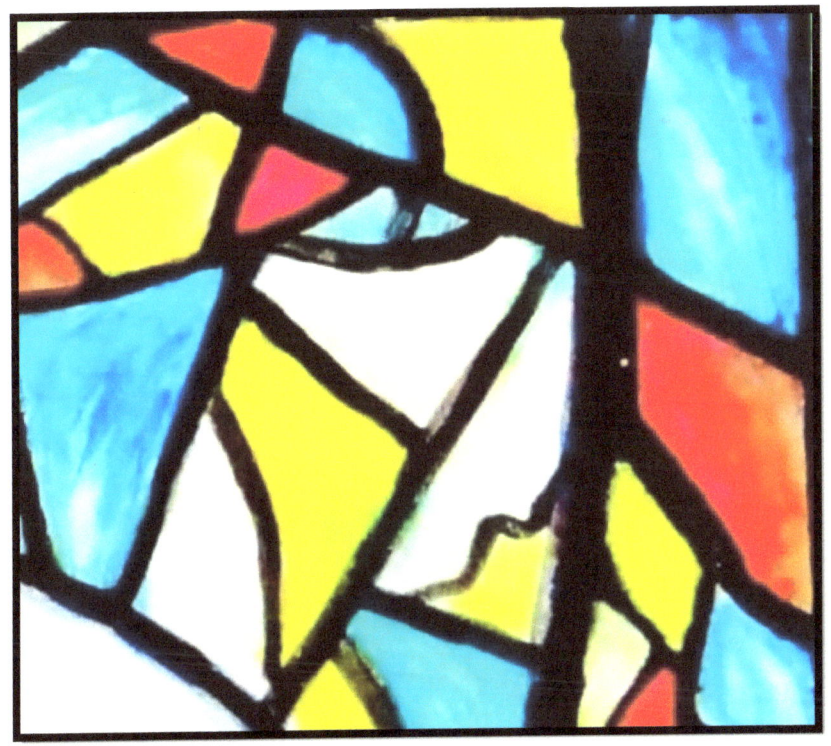

Title: abstract Stained Glass Birds, Three
Copyright by Dan Wetta

This is a small section of my painting, "Stained Glass Birds."

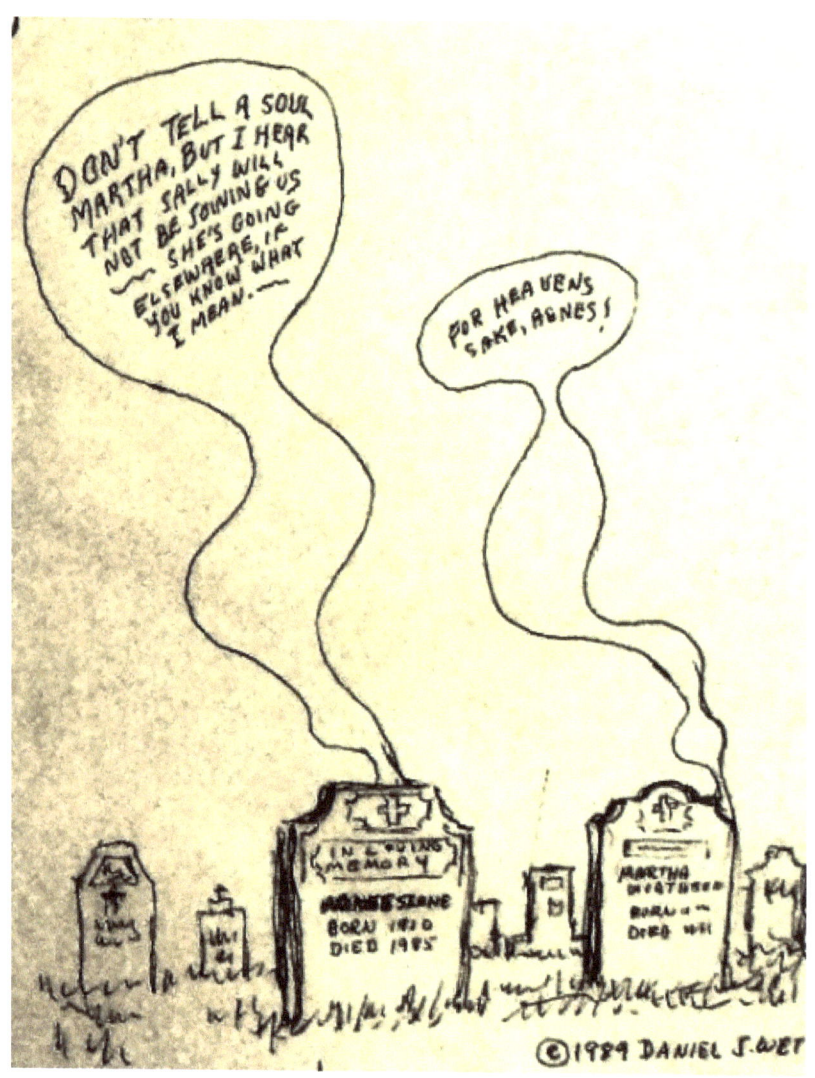

Title: Graveyard Gossip
Copyright by Dan Wetta 1989

People are in graveyards an awful long time. There is not much to do except to gossip.

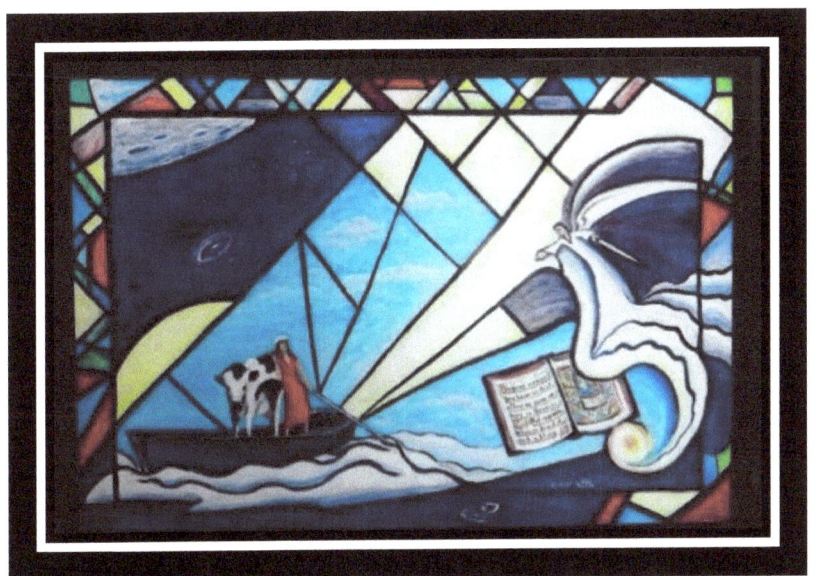

Title: What? No Cows In Heaven?
Size: 24x36 inches
Medium: Acrylic on canvas
Copyright by Dan Wetta 1995

If this lady loves her cow so much that she would take it for a ride in her row boat, surely she would want to take it to heaven with her!

But I once heard a TV preacher tell a lady that she couldn't take her little doggie to heaven with her, so they probably don't allow cows up there either.

The holy book in the following abstract from this acrylic explains all.

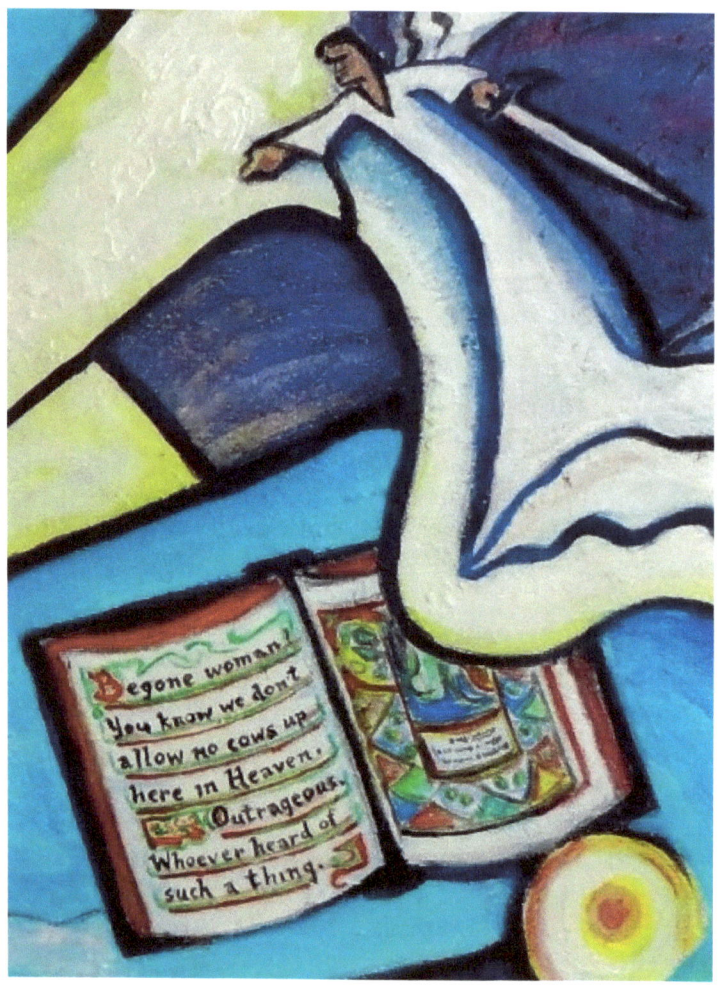

Title: excerpt from Book of No Cows
Copyright by Dan Wetta 1995

Did you ever wonder why they don't allow cows in heaven? The holy book in this abstract from my acrylic, "What? No Cows in Heaven?" explains thus:

"Begone, woman! You know we don't allow no cows up here in Heaven! Outrageous! Whoever heard of such a thing?"

Chapter 11: If You Think You Got Problems!

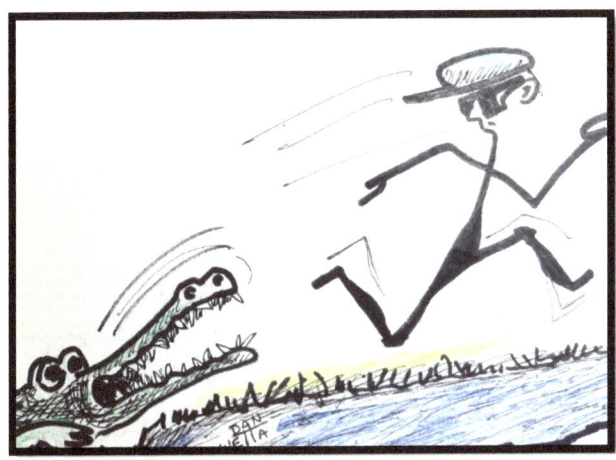

Sometimes the problems of others puts into perspective how simple or small our problems really are. In this chapter, I try to illustrate through my cartoons some of the predicaments others face.

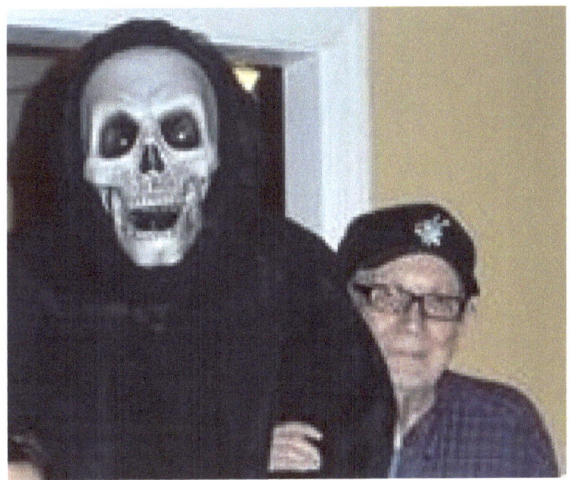

If you think I have a distorted sense of humor, don't blame me. That big Hoodie next to me is my gag writer.

There are days when I feel like this:

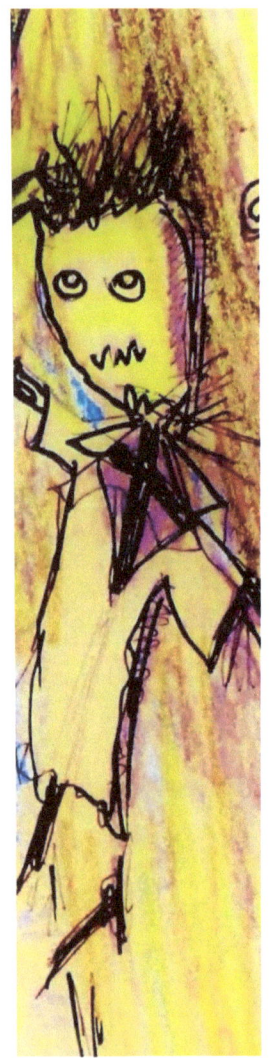

Title: If You Feel Like This
Copyright by Dan Wetta

If you feel like this, you got problems.

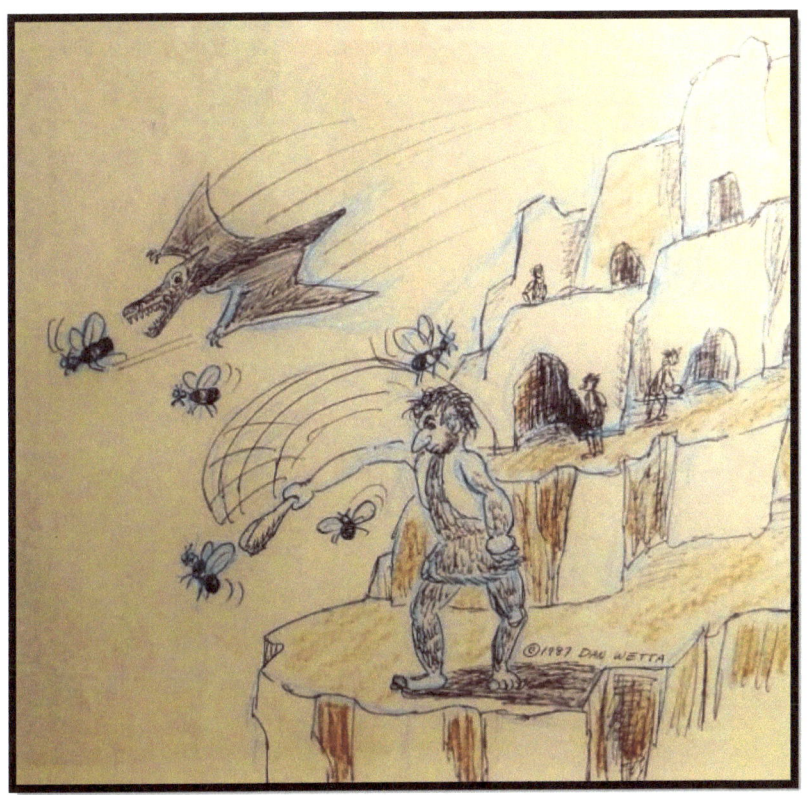

Title: Nobody Likes Flies
Copyright by Dan Wetta 1987

If you think you got problems, if life is getting you down, think about the fly. People have been trying to swat them all the way back from cave man days.

Even the cows and horses have fly swatter tails.

By the way, that's the original bat man in the sky.

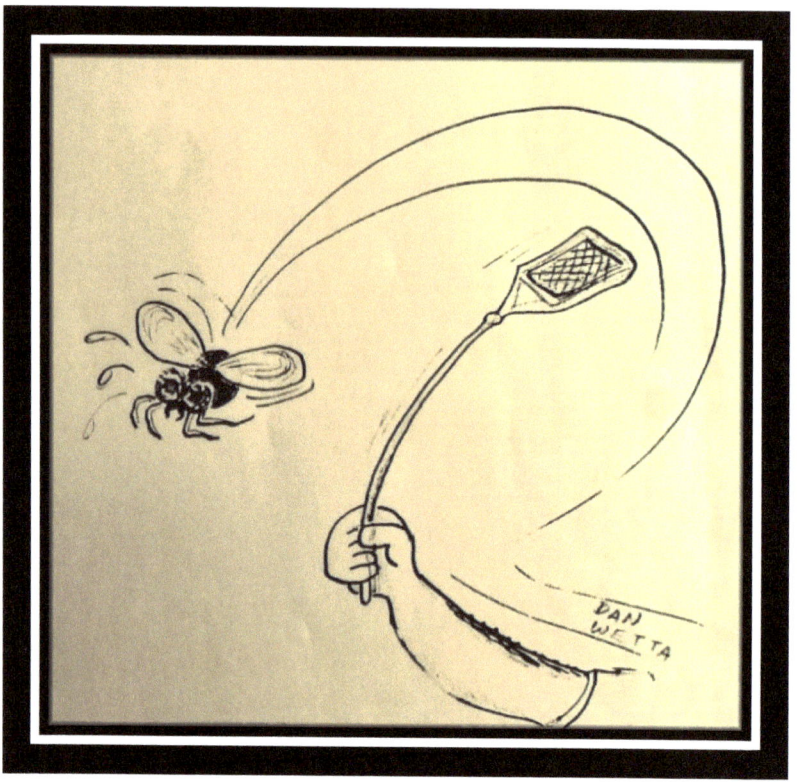

Title: No Flies in Heaven
Copyright by Dan Wetta

I don't think flies are allowed in heaven.
Just continuing the fly theme here.

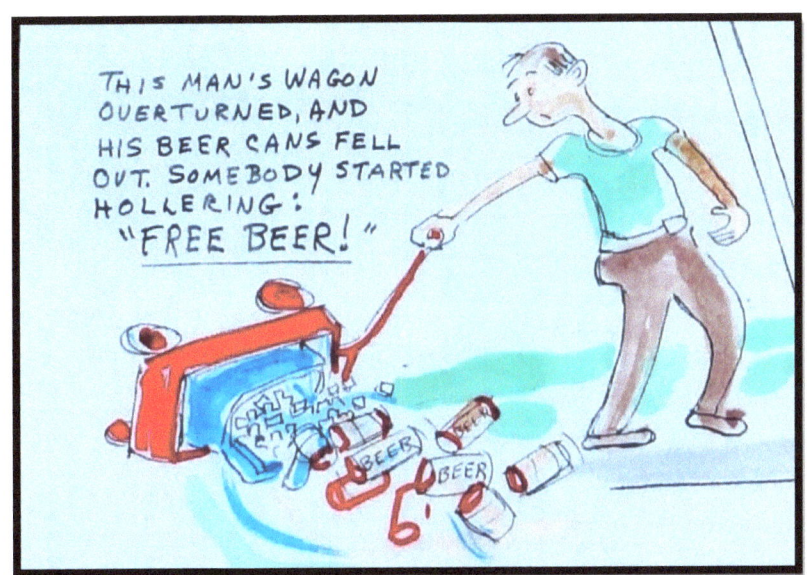

IF YOU THINK YOU GOT PROBLEMS!

Title: cartoon Free Beer
Copyright by Dan Wetta

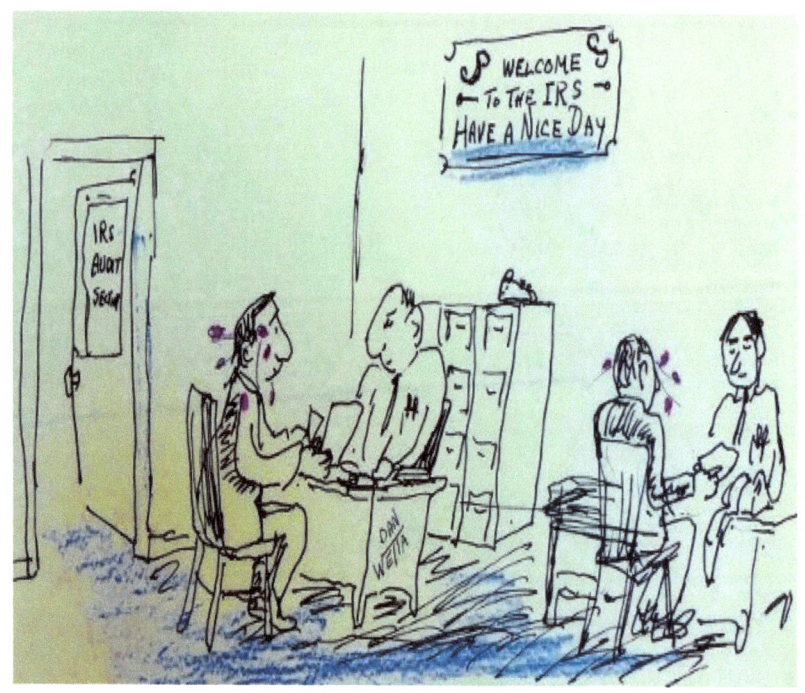

Title: Have a Nice Day
Copyright by Dan Wetta

Yeah, have a nice day sweating blood with the IRS!

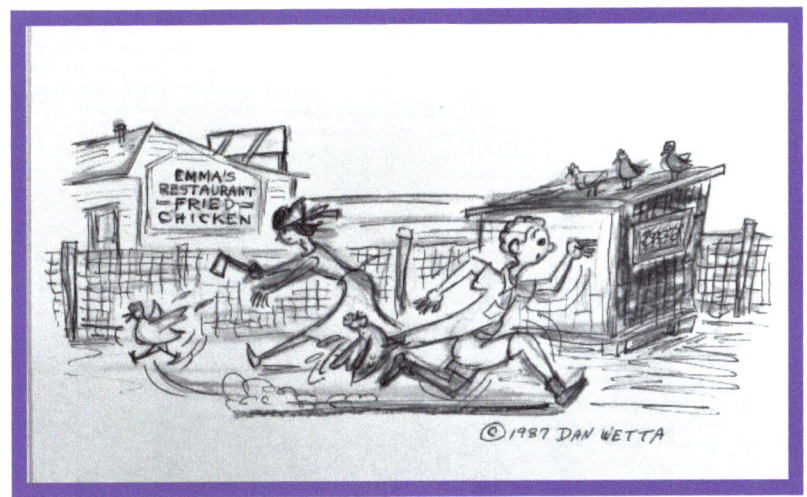

Title: Run, Chicken, Run!
Copyright by Dan Wetta 1987

Pictures like this make me glad I'm not a chicken.

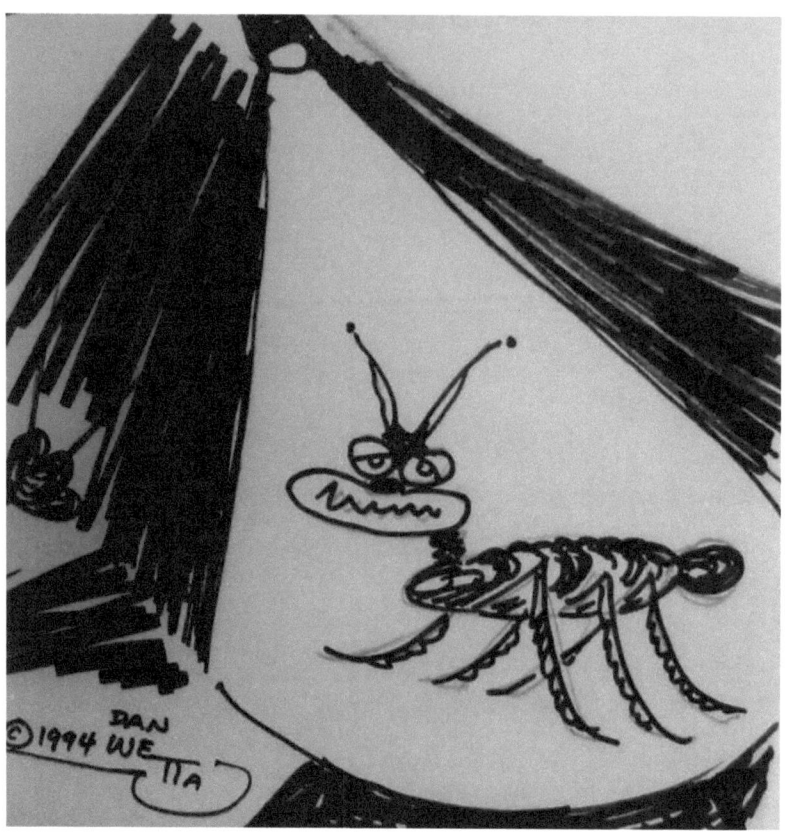

Title: In the Bug Light
Copyright by Dan Wetta 1994

The guy who invented the bug zapper must have realized that even bugs want to be in the spotlight like a Hollywood star. Sometimes it doesn't pay to be in the spotlight. You might get zapped!

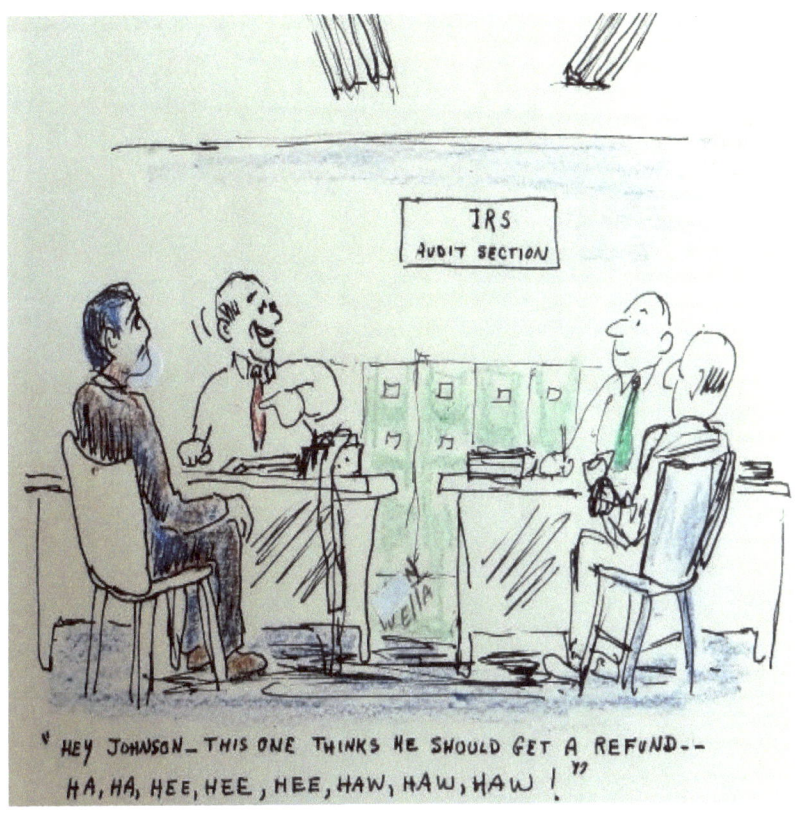

Title: Refund Haw Haw
Copyright by Dan Wetta

I think there is a color code for the ties that those two auditors are wearing.

Red-tie guys make taxpayers sweat blood, and green-tie guys rack up a lot of money on audits.

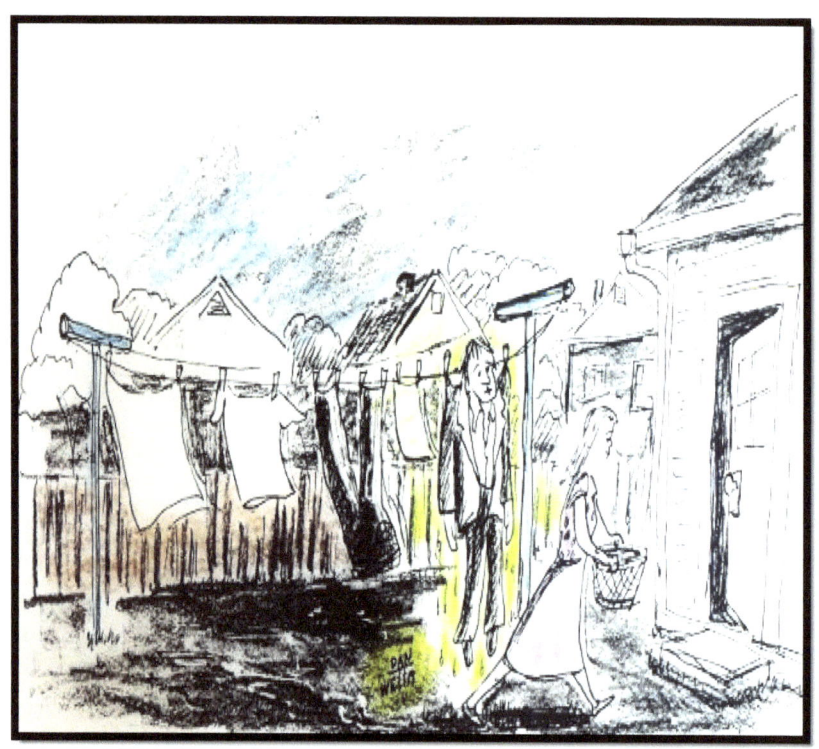

Title: Just Hanging Out
Copyright by Dan Wetta

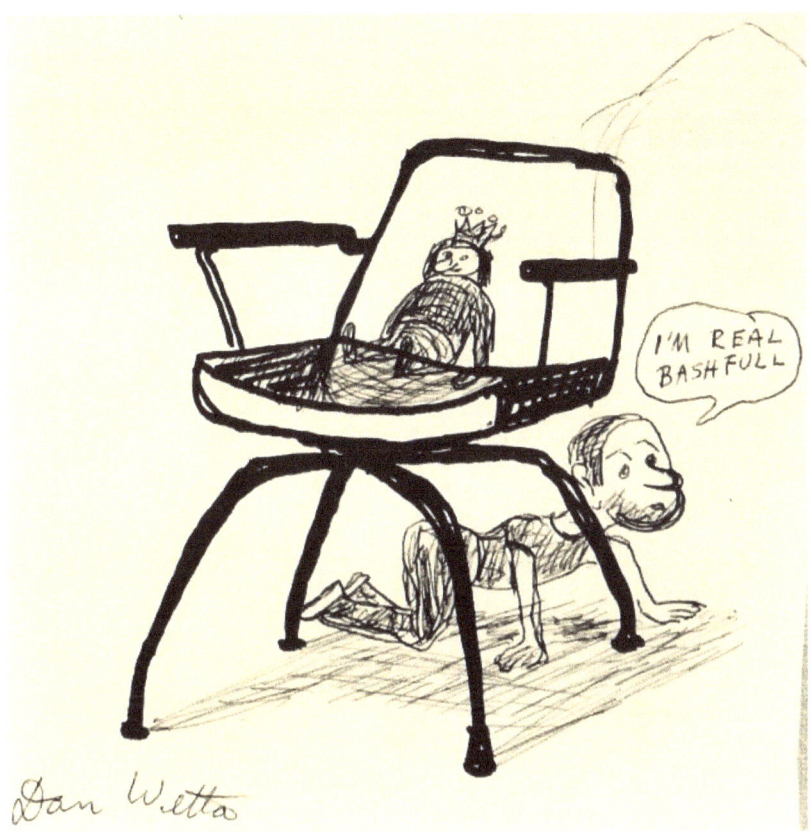

Title: Bashful
Copyright by Dan Wetta

I drew a king sitting in an ordinary chair instead of on a throne.
No wonder I'm hiding behind the chair pretending to be bashful.

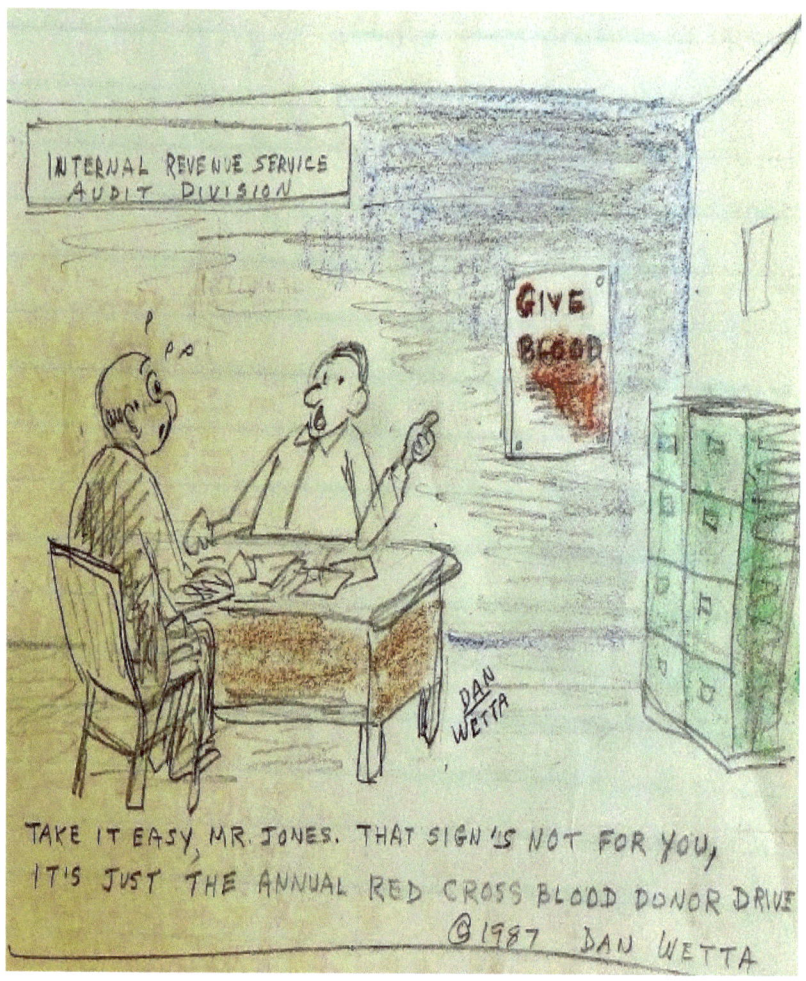

Title: Give Blood
Copyright by Dan Wetta

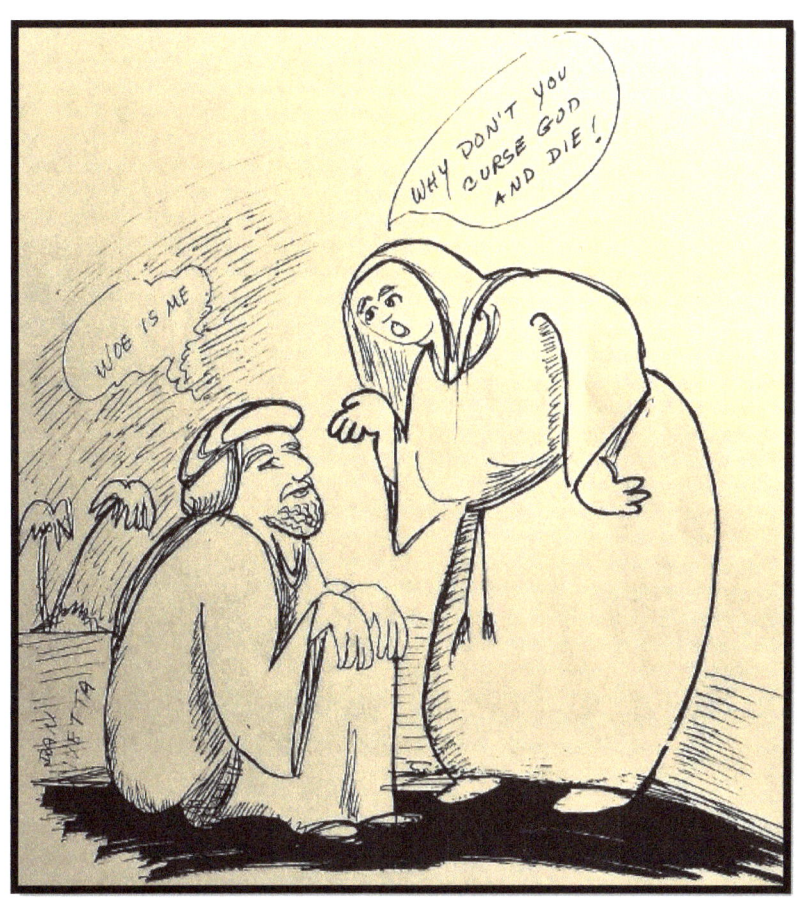

Title: Job's Wife
Copyright by Dan Wetta

When Job was down and out, his wife wanted no part of his problems. "Why don't you curse God and die!" is the wife's response to Job's, "Woe is me!"

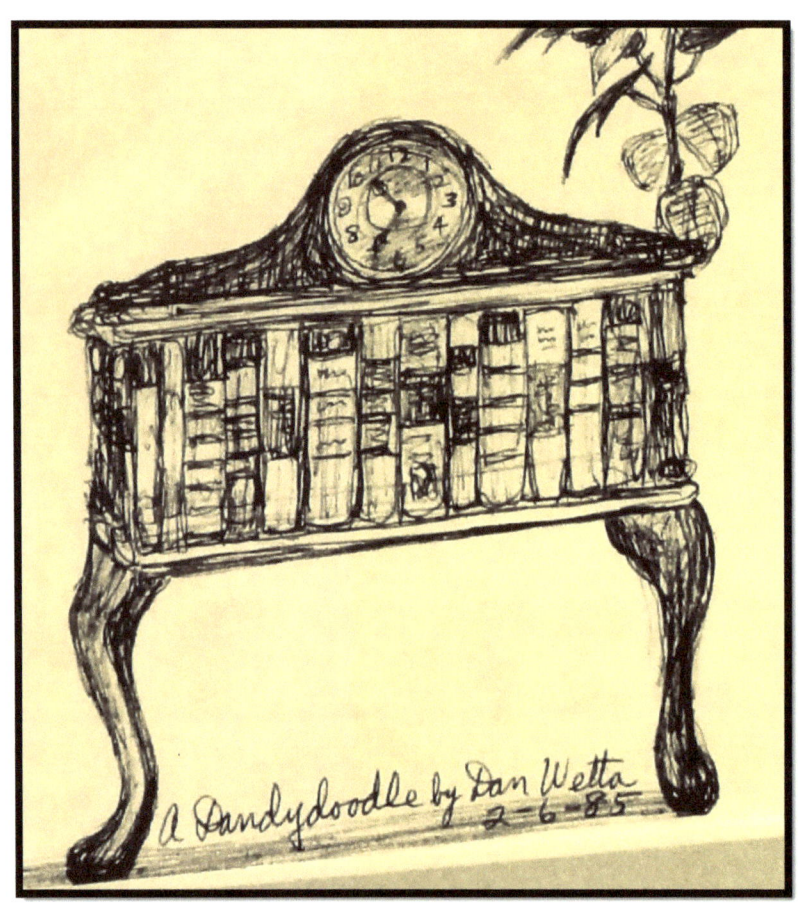

Title: Two-legged Book Case
Copyright by Dan Wetta 1985

You think you got problems?
This two-legged book case has to do a balancing act twenty four hours a day!

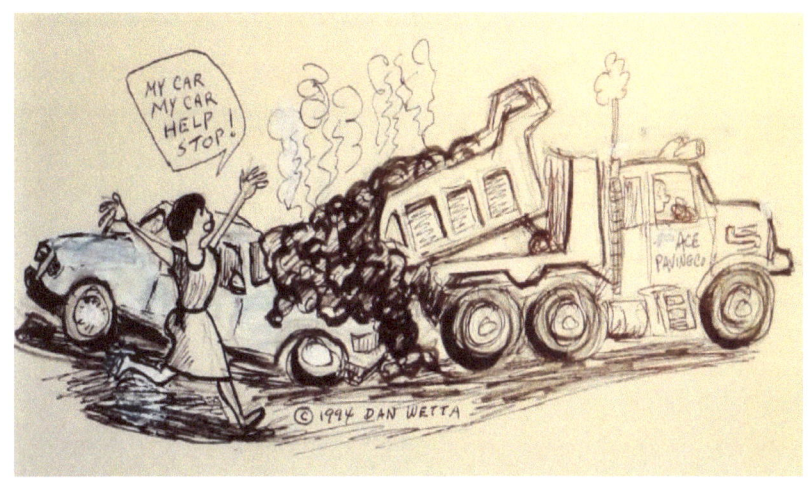

Title: Help! Stop!
Copyright by Dan Wetta 1994

Things like this do happen sometimes.

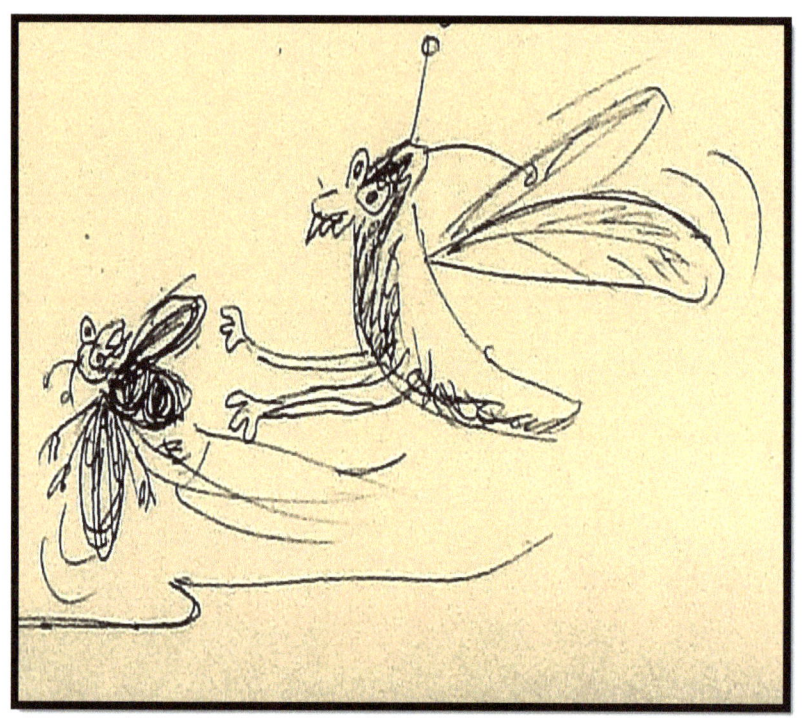

Title: Bug eat Bug
Copyright by Dan Wetta

When a big bug is chasing you, you got a problem.

Chapter 12: Motherly Visions

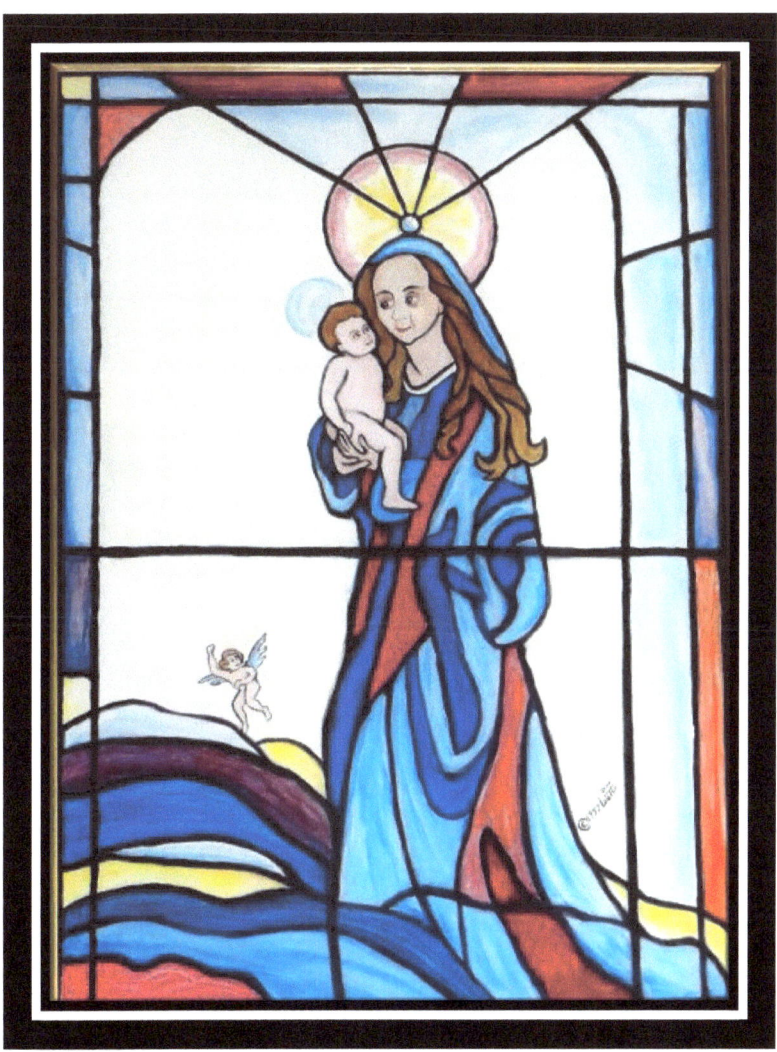

Title: Motherly Vision
Size: 22x36 inches
Medium: Acrylic on canvas
Copyright by Dan Wetta 1997

Years ago, we had a family reunion. All of us were in the living room talking and laughing about the good times we used to have as kids in New Orleans.

I happened to look up, and there was my mother standing in the doorway with a smile on her face. She was so pleased to see that all her children were grown up and happily married. At that moment, none of us seemed to have problems.

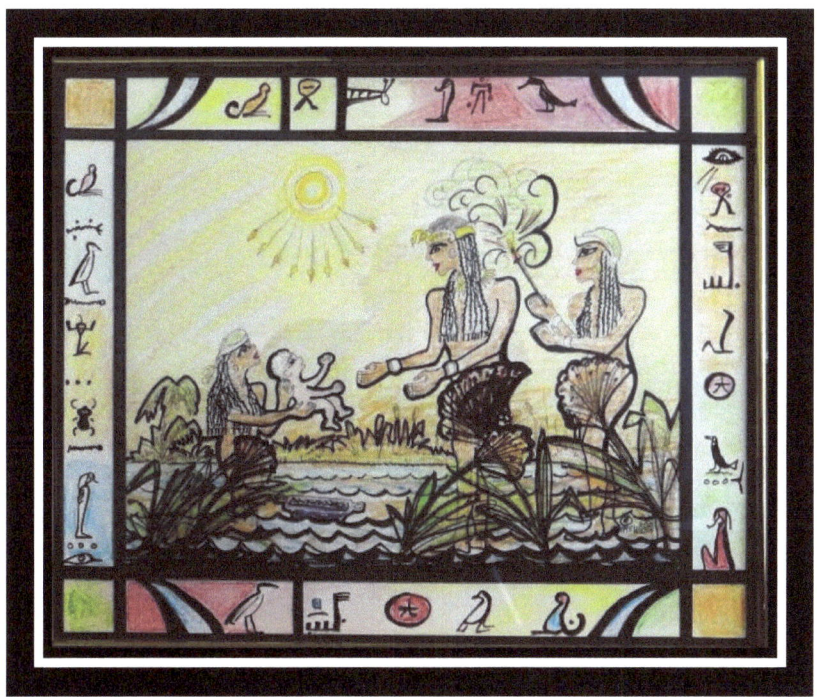

Pharaoh's Daughter Rescues Moses
Size: 16x20 inches
Medium: Mixed media on paper
Copyright by Dan Wetta 1995

And speaking of mothers:

Moses' mother concocted a scheme to save baby Moses, whom Pharaoh wanted dead. Pharaoh of Egypt had ordered that all Hebrew baby boys should be thrown into the Nile River, but that all baby girls should live.

Moses' mother hid him for three months, but when she could hide him no longer, she put him in a basket coated with tar and pitch and hid it among the reeds along the bank of the Nile River. Moses's sister stood at a distance to see what would happen.

Pharaoh's daughter went down to the Nile to bathe, and she saw the basket among the reeds. She sent her slave girl to get it. Baby

Moses was crying and she felt sorry for him. "This is one of the Hebrew babies." she said.

Then Moses' sister asked Pharaoh's daughter if she should go get one of the Hebrew women to nurse the baby.

"Yes, go" she answered, and Moses' sister went and got Moses' mother, who took care of him until he got older.

Then she brought Moses to Pharaoh's daughter, and he became her son.

Even if you are a bible skeptic, you should read the full story in Exodus 2.

It is one of the greatest Mother's Day stories ever told.

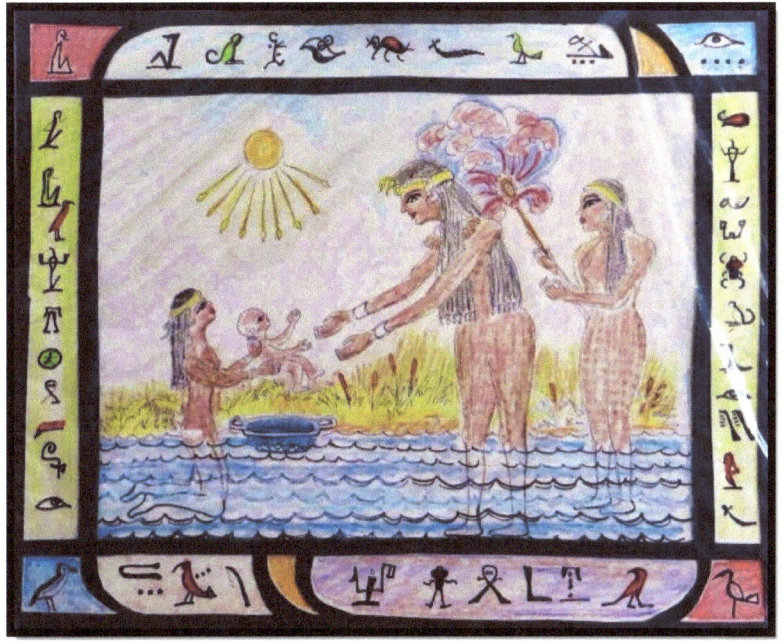

Title: Pharaoh's Daughter and Baby Moses
Copyright by Dan Wetta

I did two versions of Pharaoh's Daughter rescuing baby Moses.

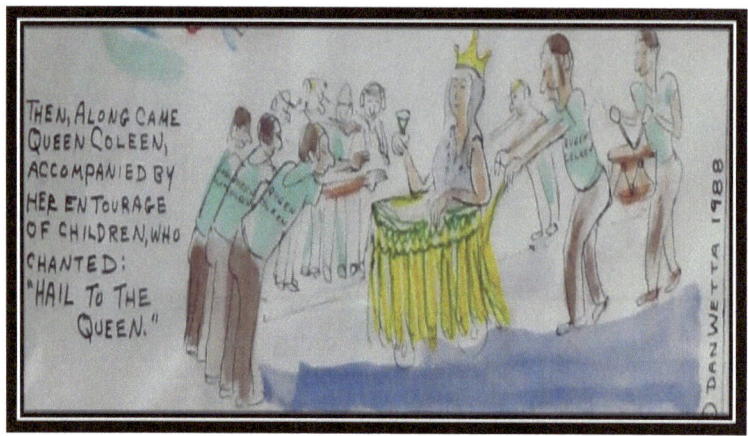

Title: Queen Coleen
Copyright by Dan Wetta 1988

This is an excerpt from my cartoon, "Only In New Orleans."

Every year at Mardi Gras time in New Orleans, Coleen's sons get together to honor their mother in their neighborhood parade.

They decorate a grocery shopping cart like a float for their mother and march her up and down the parade route before the parade begins.

Chapter 13: Stairway to Heaven

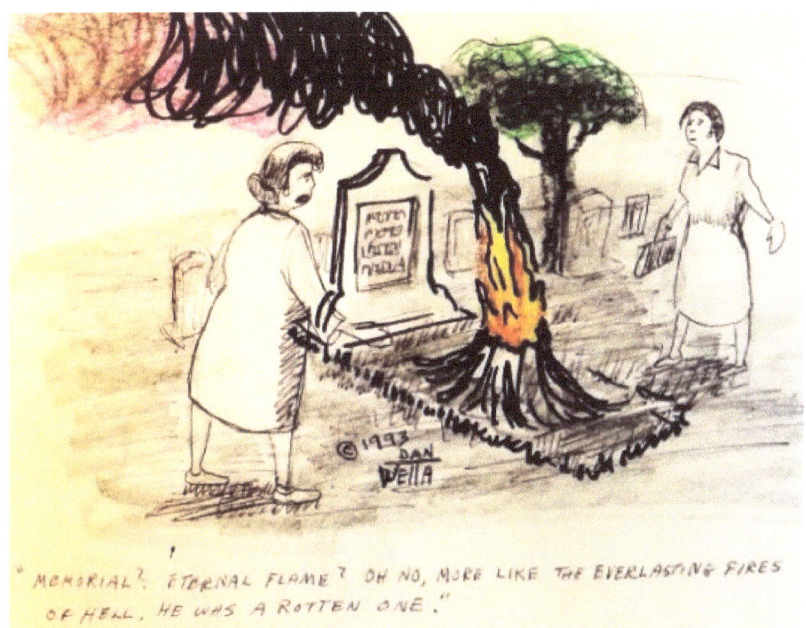

"Memorial? Eternal Flame? Oh no, more like the everlasting fires of hell. He was a rotten one!"

Title: Eternal Flame
Copyright by Dan Wetta 1993

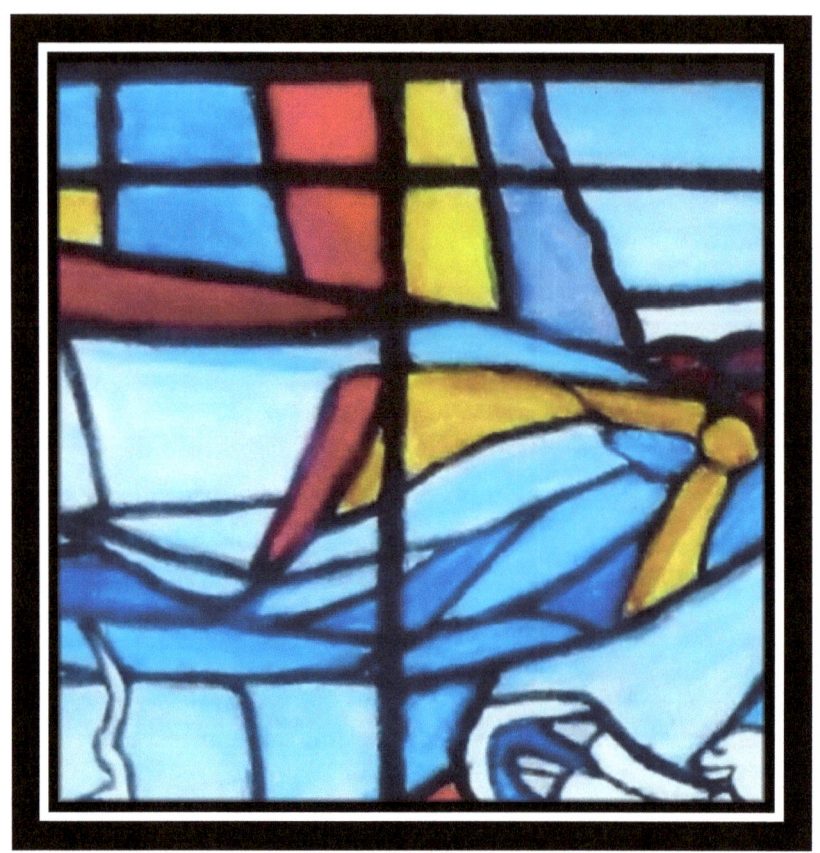

Abstract Lost Lamb
Copyright by Dan Wetta 1997

This was taken from my painting, "Lost Lamb.

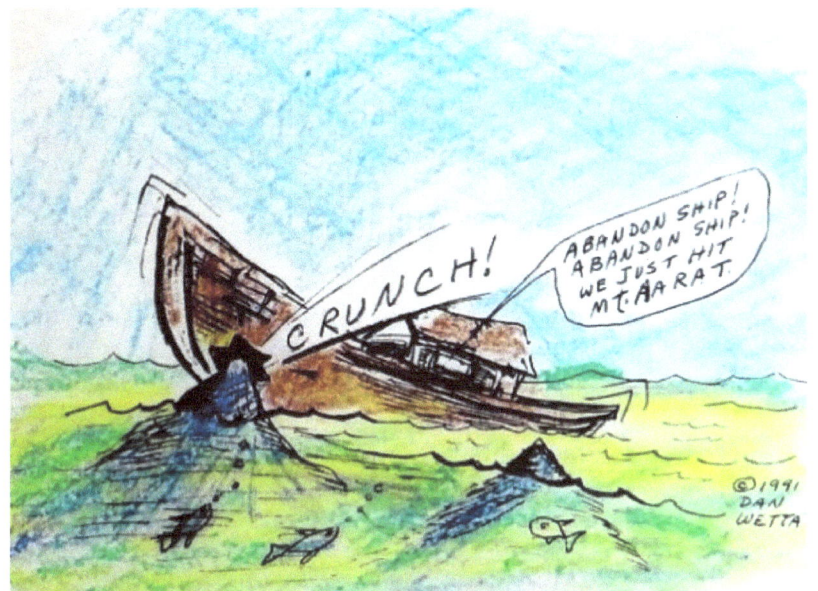

Title: Abandon Ship
Copyright by Dan Wetta 1991

A fateful day aboard Noah's ark.

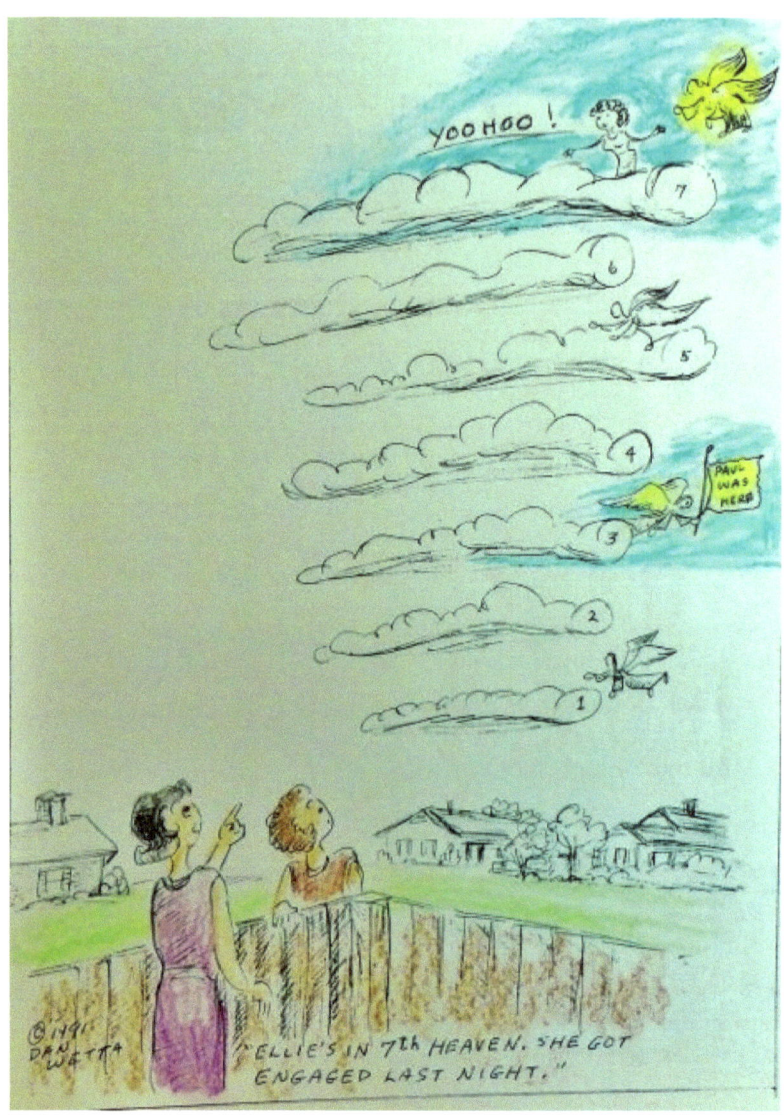

Title: Seventh Heaven
Copyright by Dan Wetta 1991

The woman is saying, "Ellie's in 7th heaven! She got engaged last night." You can see Ellie on the seventh level as she yells, "Yoo-hoo!" while an angel blows a trumpet.

Another angel carries a flag on the third level proclaiming, "Paul was here."

In 2 Corinthians 12:2, Paul says that he was caught up to the third heaven, but he did not die to get there.

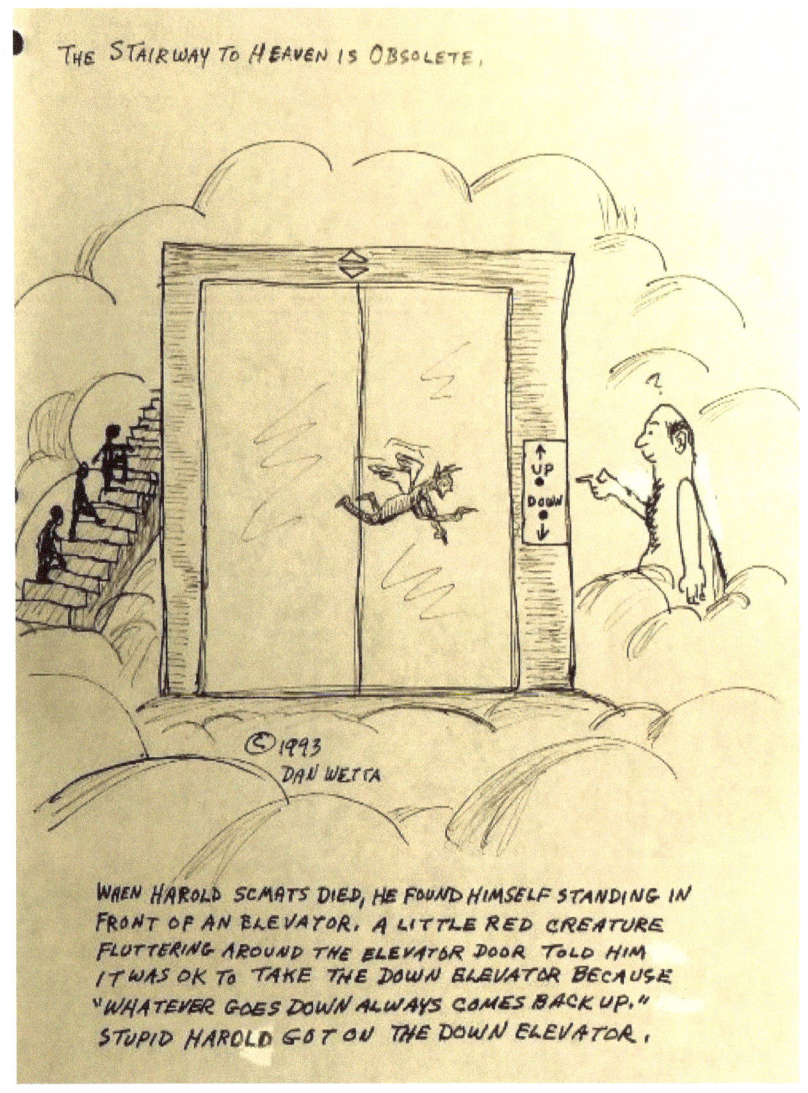

Title: Press the Down Button
Copyright by Dan Wetta 1993

Chapter 14: Ponderings of Bible and Evolution

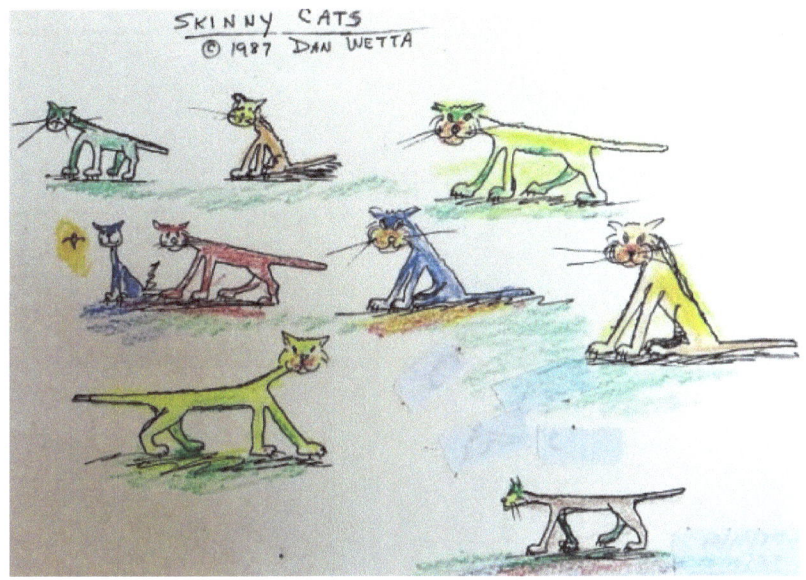

Title: Skinny Cats
Copyright by Dan Wetta 1987

This cartoon is included in my book, An Artist's Life, along with the following two, because these go with the theme of this chapter.

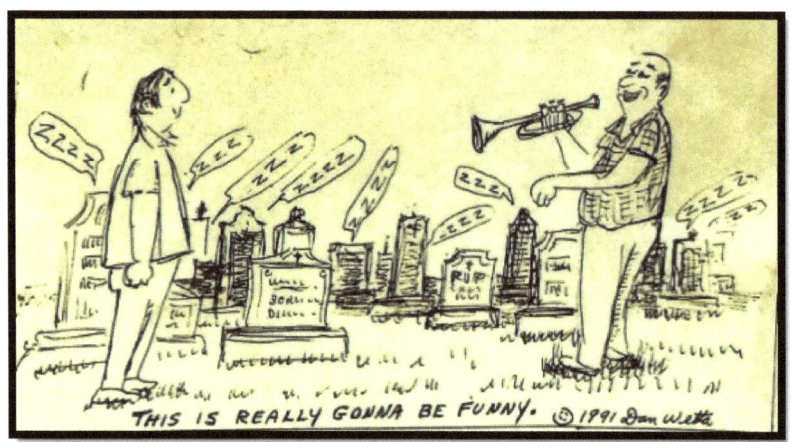

"This is really gonna be funny."

Title: Graveyard Bugler
Copyright by Dan Wetta 1991

They would both do you-know-what in their pants if those dead souls did arise from their graves.

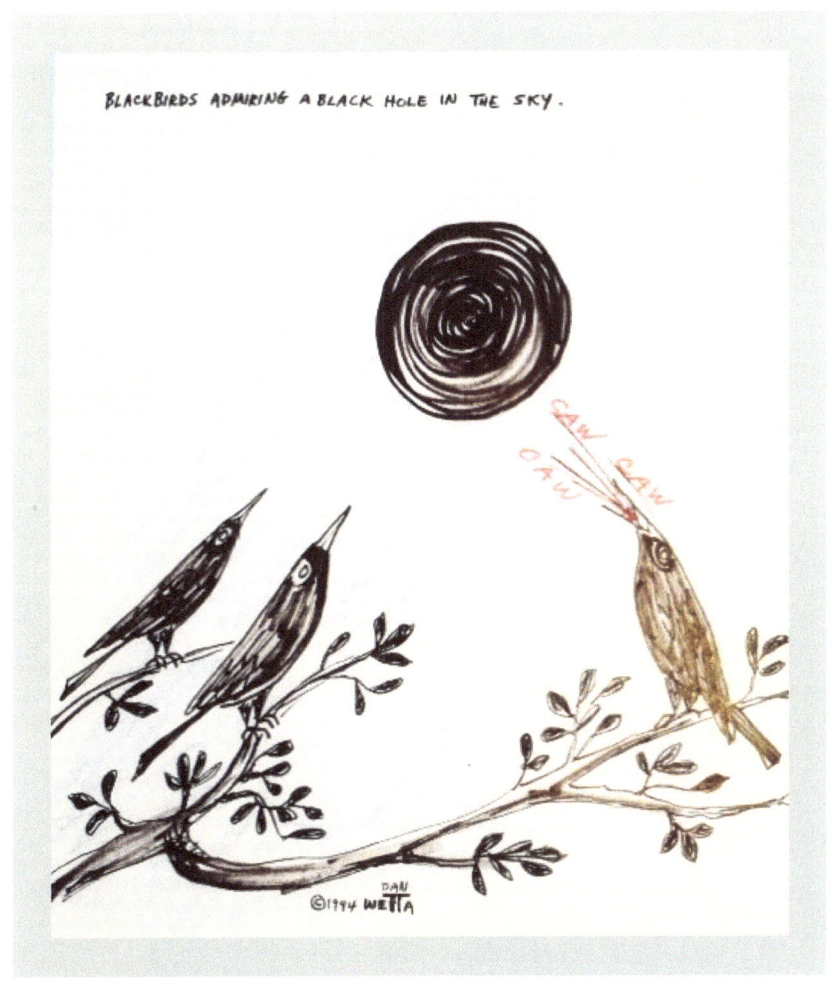

Title: Two Black Birds Admire Black Hole in Sky
Copyright by Dan Wetta

But the brown bird thinks it is funny.

The Spanish laugh is ja ja ja; the gringo laugh is ha ha ha; the Santa Claus laugh is ho ho ho; a belly laugh is haw haw, haw; and the brown bird laugh is caw caw caw.

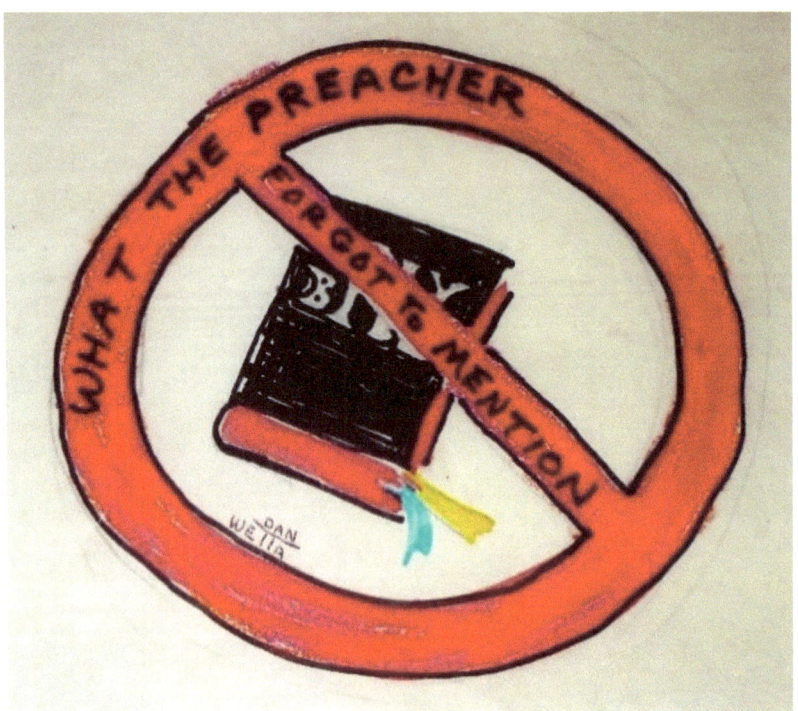

Title: What the Preacher Forgot to Mention

In my first E-book, *Sometimes I Can Be a Smart Aleck*, I said that I could not find anything wrong with the Bible except for man's interpretation of it. Five bible scholars can read the same passage in the Bible and come up with five different interpretations of it.

Let's make that six, because I don't think that any bible scholar or preacher would envision the Bible stories in the ways that my cartoons do.

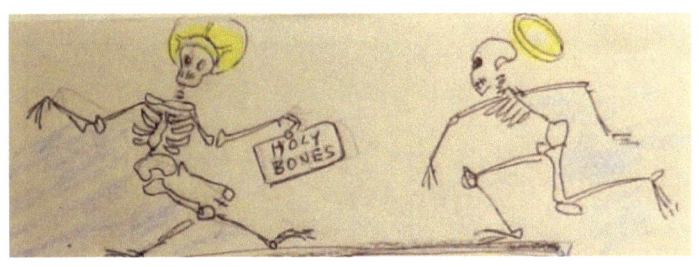

Title: cartoon Valley of Dry Bones
Copyright by Dan Wetta

Preachers don't talk too much about chapter 37 of the prophet Ezekiel. However, a song writer was inspired to write a song about dry bones coming back to life, and I was inspired to do this cartoon when I read chapter 37 of Ezekiel.

In fact, it also led me to do a lot of skeleton and graveyard cartoons, so it's probably a good thing I did not become a preacher, because instead of preaching a sermon, I would be up at the podium showing pictures of my skeleton gags to the congregation.

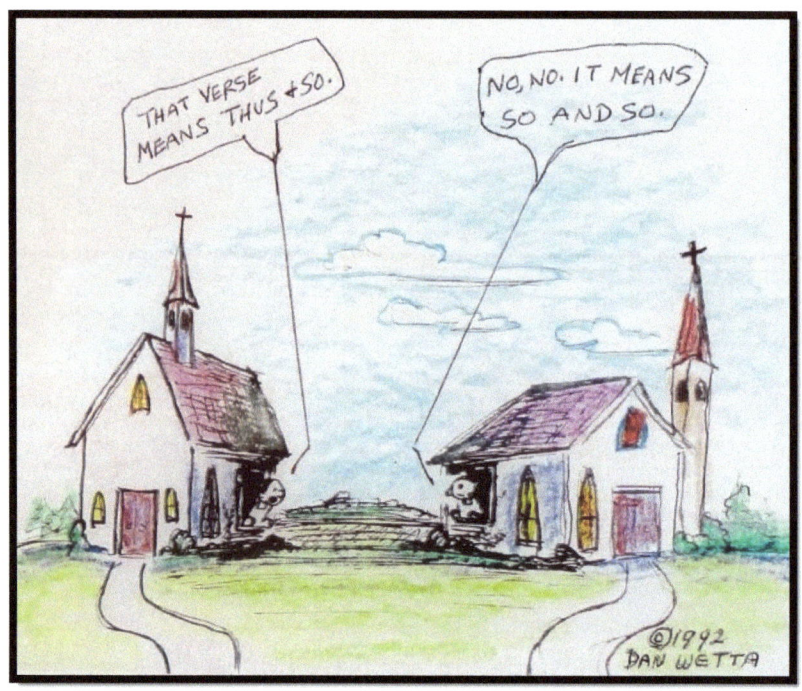

Title: Church Splits
Copyright by Dan Wetta 1992

The problem is not with scripture, but churches have split into various denominations because of differences in the interpretation or meaning of scripture.

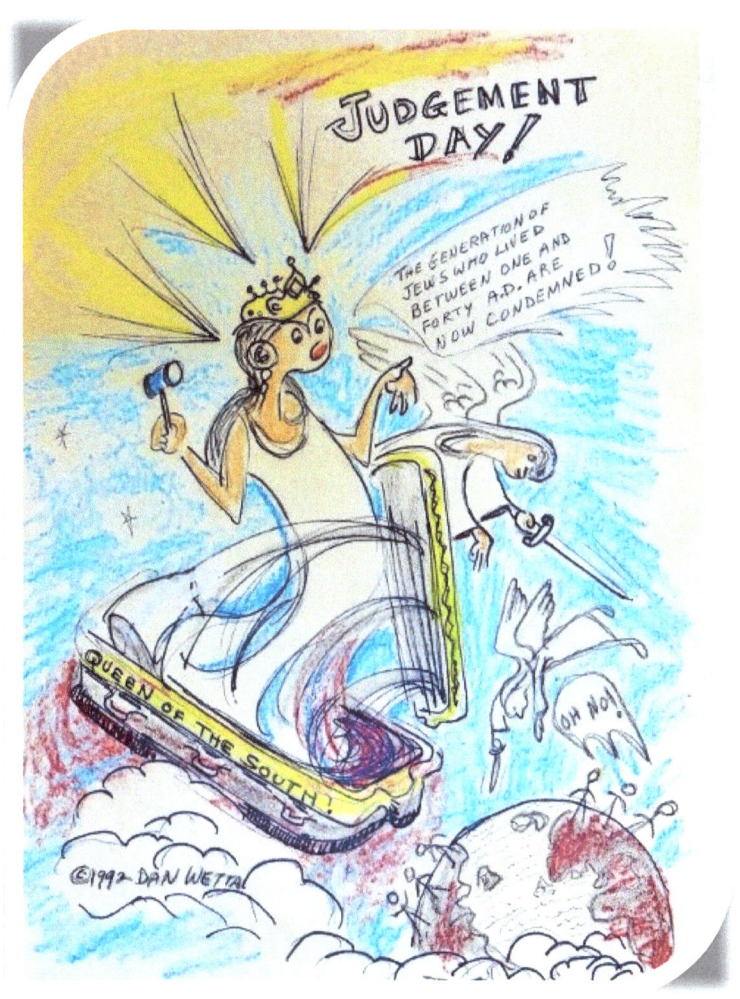

Title: Queen of the South
Copyright by Dan Wetta 1992

Judgment Day! The generation of Jews who lived between One and Forty A.D. are now condemned!

Have you ever heard a preacher explain this passage, Mt:12:42?:

"The Queen of the South will rise at the judgment with this generation and condemn it; for she came from the ends of the earth to listen to Solomon's wisdom, and now one greater than Solomon is here."

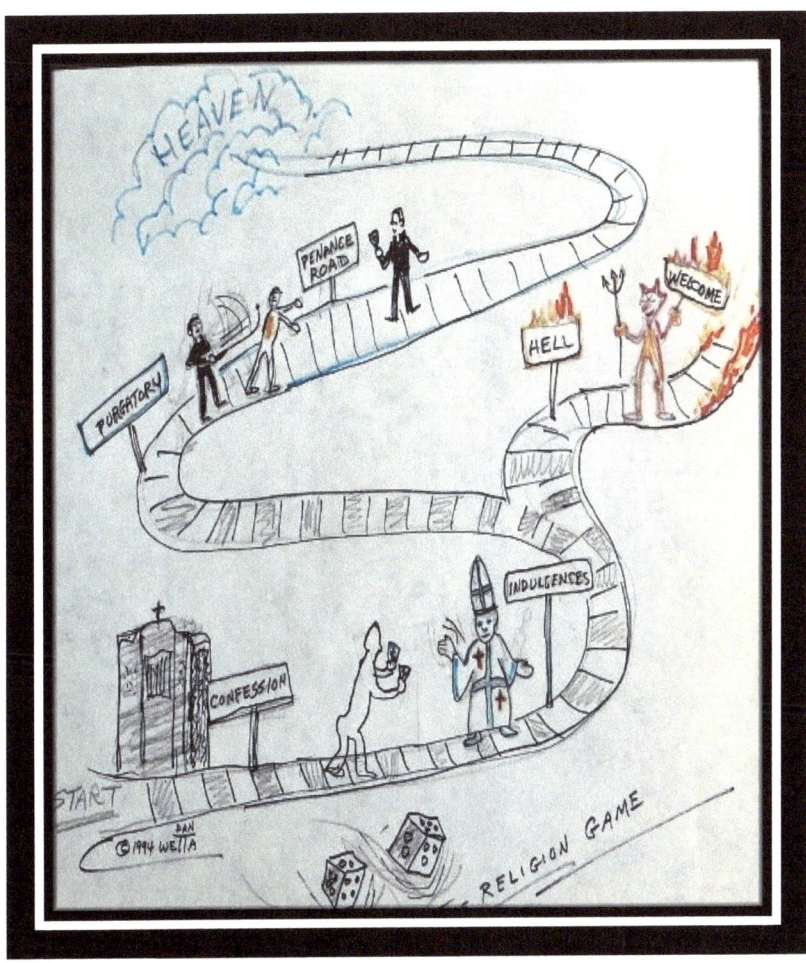

Title: Game of Religion
Copyright by Dan Wetta 1994

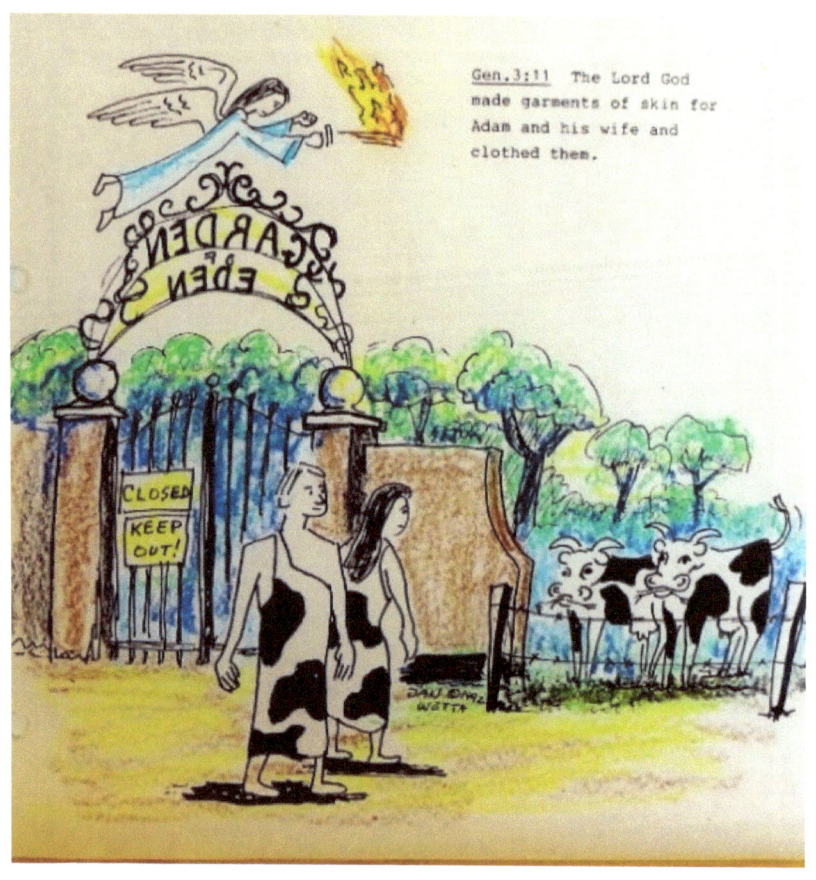

Gen.3:11 The Lord God made garments of skin for Adam and his wife and clothed them.

Title: Garments of Skin
Copyright by Dan Wetta1992

Genesis 3:11: "The Lord God made garments of skin for Adam and his wife and clothed them."

I did a different version of this as a night scene, using acrylic on canvas. It is in one of my other books.

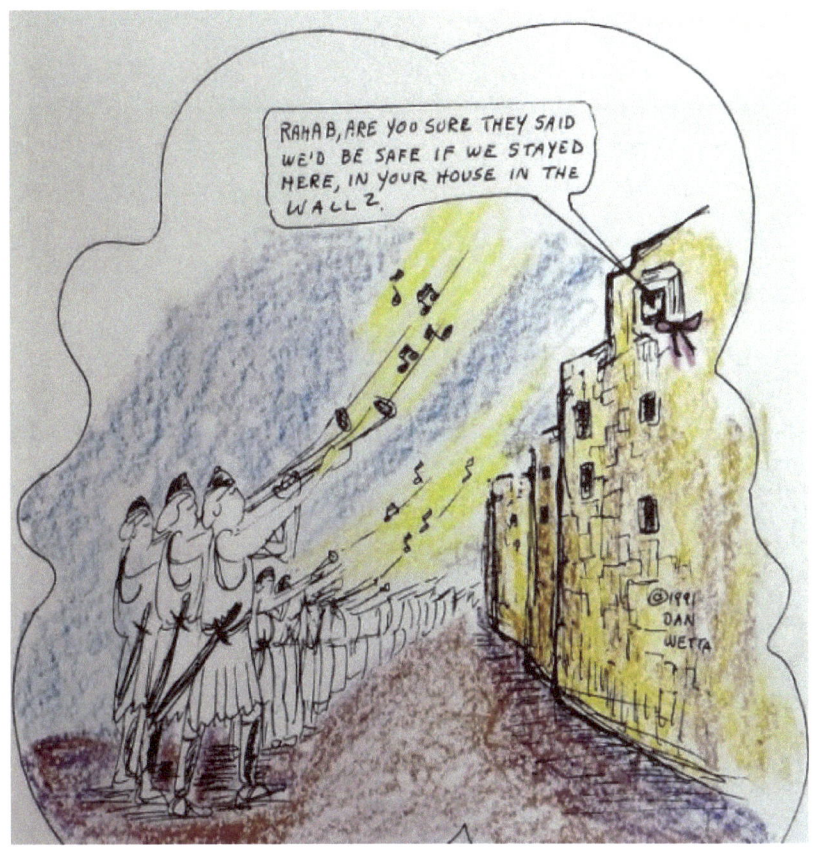

Title: Jericho
Copyright by Dan Wetta 1991

Rahab and the Wall of Jericho

Rahab was a prostitute who lived in a house that was part of the city wall of Jericho. When Joshua sent two spies to reconnoiter the city, she hid them in her house, and later on she lowered them down by a rope through the window. The spies had promised safety for her and her entire family if they stayed in the house when they came back to destroy the city, and she tied a scarlet cord in the window. See Joshua 2:15.

A few days later:

Josh.6:20-25

The army of Israel marched around Jericho seven times. Then they blew the trumpets and when the trumpets sounded and all the people shouted, the wall collapsed; so every man charged straight in, and they took the city. Joshua said to the two men who had spied out the land, "Go into the prostitute's house and bring her out and all who belong to her."

Something else the preacher forgot to mention - Rahab's house was in the wall that collapsed!

Title: Jericho Text

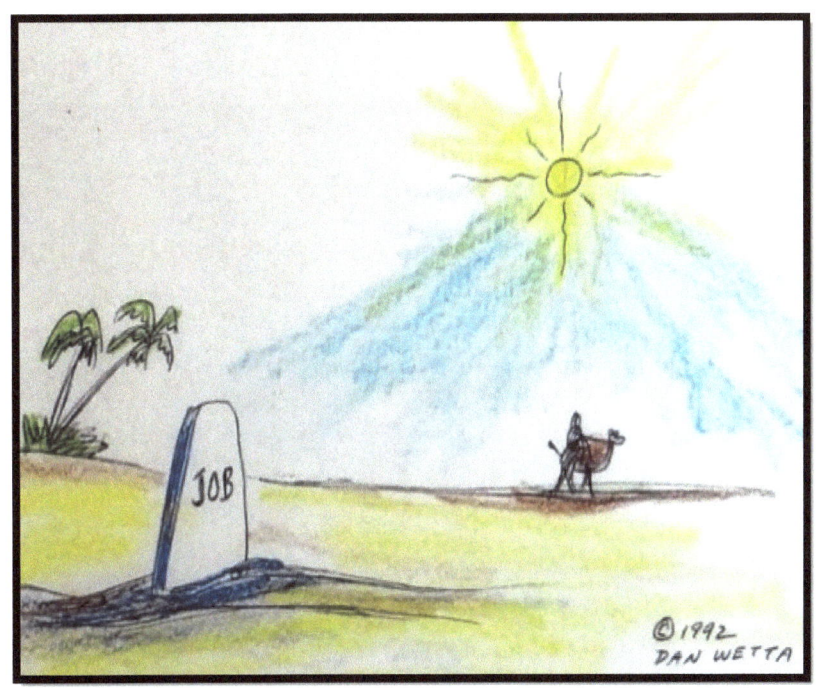

Title: Job's Tomb
Copyright by Dan Wetta 1992

```
                    Job 19:25-27

I know that my defender lives and that in

the end he will stand on my grave. And after

my flesh has been destroyed, though this

body has been destroyed, then apart from my

flesh I will see God; I myself will see him

with my own eyes - I and not another.


Job did not believe in a resurrection, but he did think he would

somehow see God 'with his own eyes' after he died.
```

Title: Text for Job's Tomb

When things weren't going well for my dad, he used to say, "I have the curse of Job."

He had a few other sayings:

"You can't beat city hall."

"If you can't beat 'em, join 'em.'"

He also thought the world was going to end in the 1940's. Well, it did end for a lot of people who got in the way of Nazi Germany.

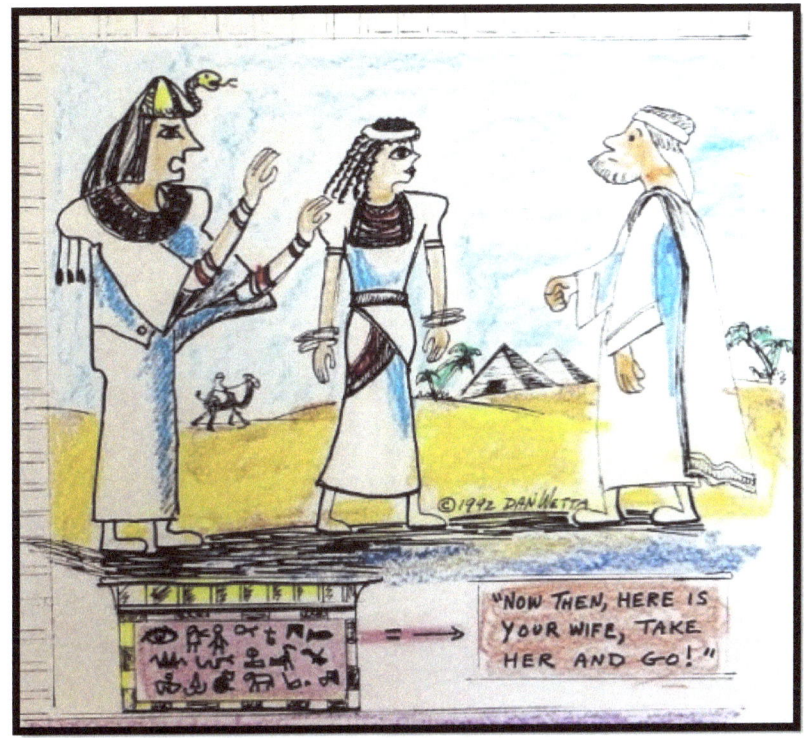

Title: Here is your Wife
Copyright by Dan Wetta 1992

Gen.12:10-20

condensed

Now there was a famine in the land, and Abraham went down to Egypt to live there for awhile because the famine was severe. As he was about to enter Egypt, he said to his wife Sarah, "I know what a beautiful woman you are. When the Egyptians see you, they will say, 'This is his wife.' Then they will kill me but let you live. Say you are my sister, so that I will be treated well for your sake and my life will be spared because of you."

. . .

Sarah was taken into Pharaoh's palace to be his wife, and then . . . Pharaoh summoned Abraham. "What have you done to me?" he said. "Why didn't you tell me she was your wife? Why did you say, 'She is my sister,' so that I took her to be my wife? Now then, here is your wife. Take her and go!"

Title: Text for "Sarah and Abraham"
This is the explanation of "Here is your wife."

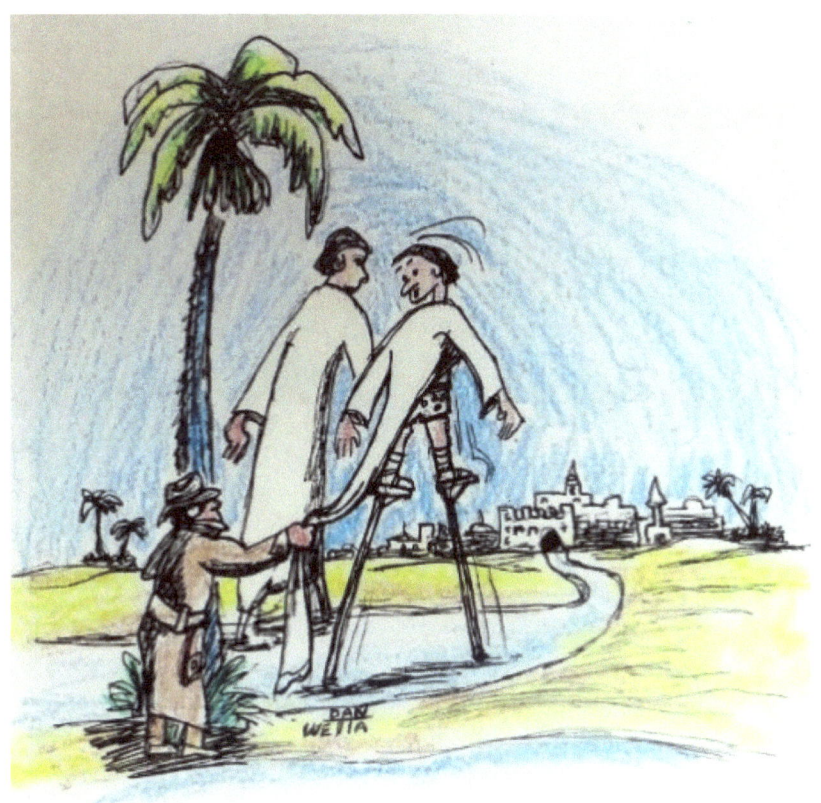

Title: Giants in Canaan
Copyright by Dan Wetta

In chapter 13 of the book of Numbers, the men who went to spy in the land of Canaan came back and told Moses, "All the people we saw there are of great size. We saw the Nephilim there." The Nephilim were giants.

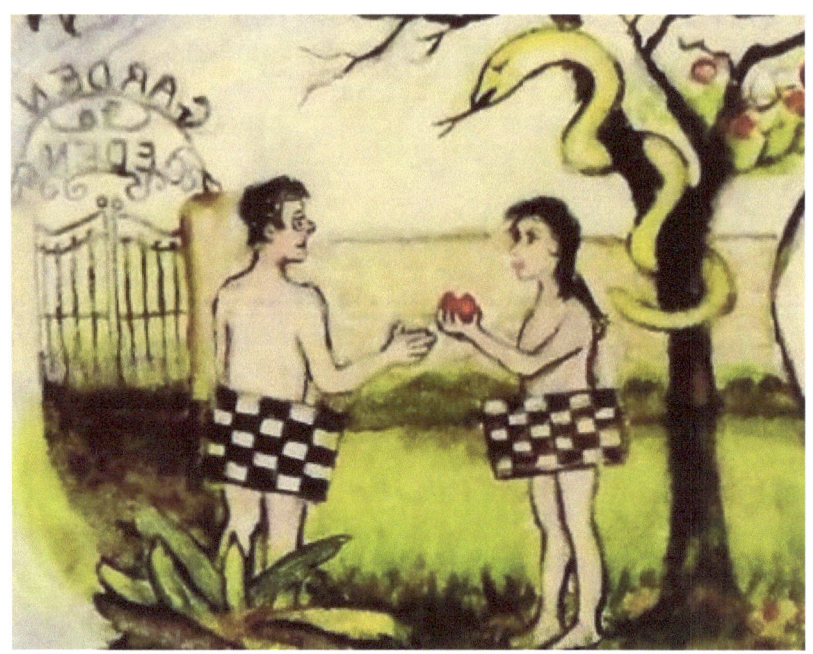

Title: Adam's Apple
Size: 10 x 12 inches
Medium: Mixed media on paper
Copyright by Dan Wetta

I have done several versions of the temptation in the Garden of Eden.

Do you remember old time TV where they used a checker board to blot out unwanted portions of the TV picture?

If you do, you are probably retired by now.

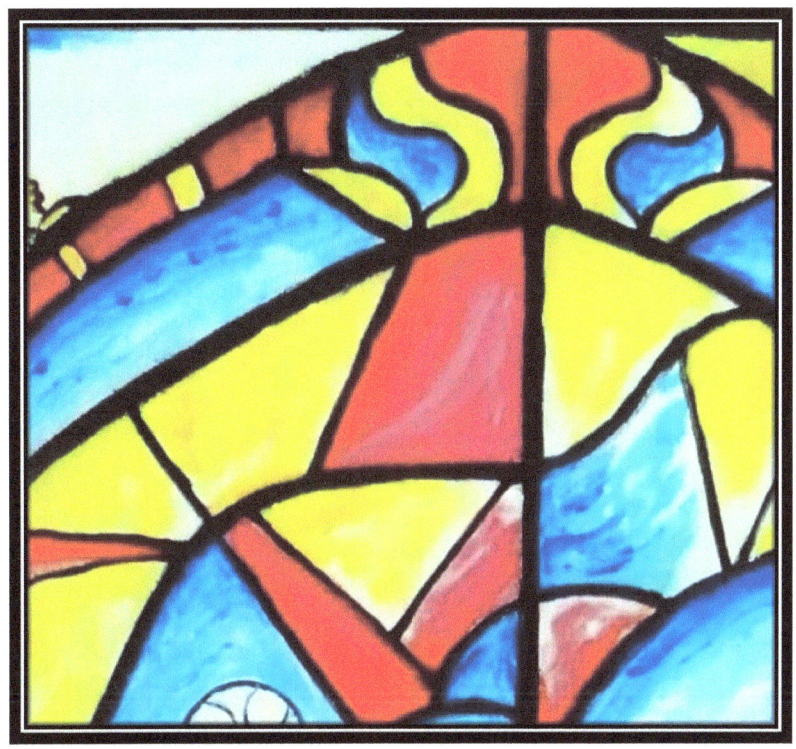

Abstract Daniel in Lions' Den
Copyright by Dan Wetta 1998

Throughout my books, I have randomly posted abstracts from larger pieces of art in my collection. This one was taken from my painting, "Daniel in Lions' Den." I never thought of myself as a painter in abstract art, but these small details have opened my eyes to the fact that I have been using abstract concepts.

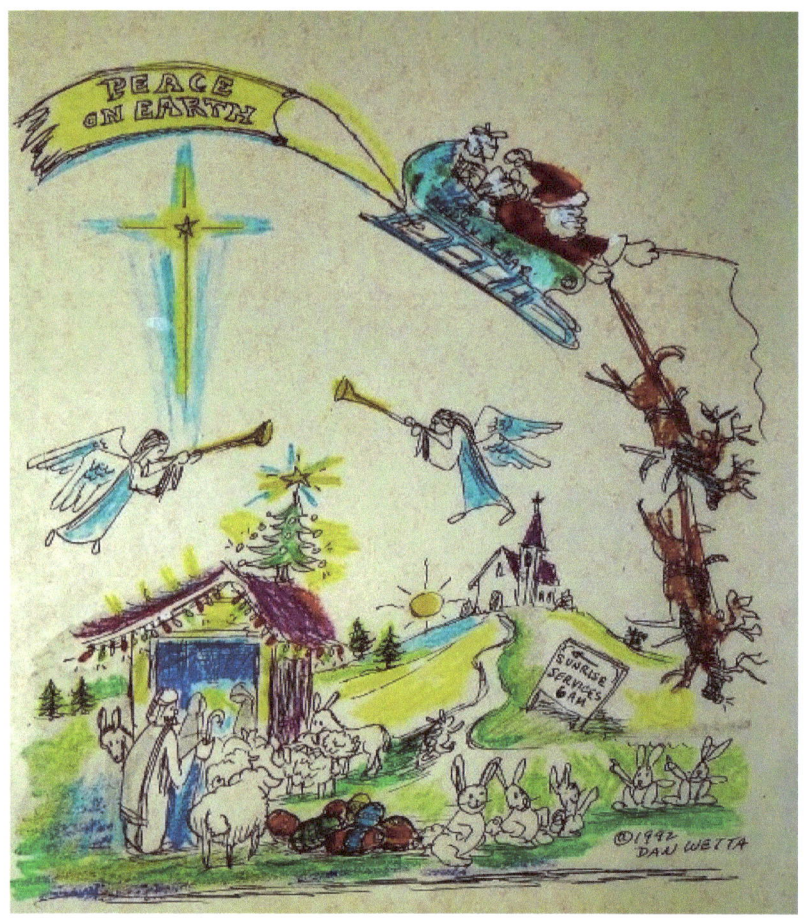

Title: Evolution of Christmas and Easter
Copyright by Dan Wetta 1992

Maybe this cartoon will shock church-goers into realizing what they have done to their two most holy days of the year, but I doubt it.

Before children hear about the baby Jesus in Sunday school, parents tell their toddlers all about Santa Claus at the North Pole and about Easter bunnies. Churches close Easter Sunday with an Easter egg hunt. Even though the children eventually realize these are all myths, the fantasy remains in their subconscious forever. No preacher does anything about it, because he or she too has been brain-washed with the myth.

The cartoon might have been viewed as sacrilegious two thousand years ago. I think it depicts the degeneration of religion since people began to believe in evolution.

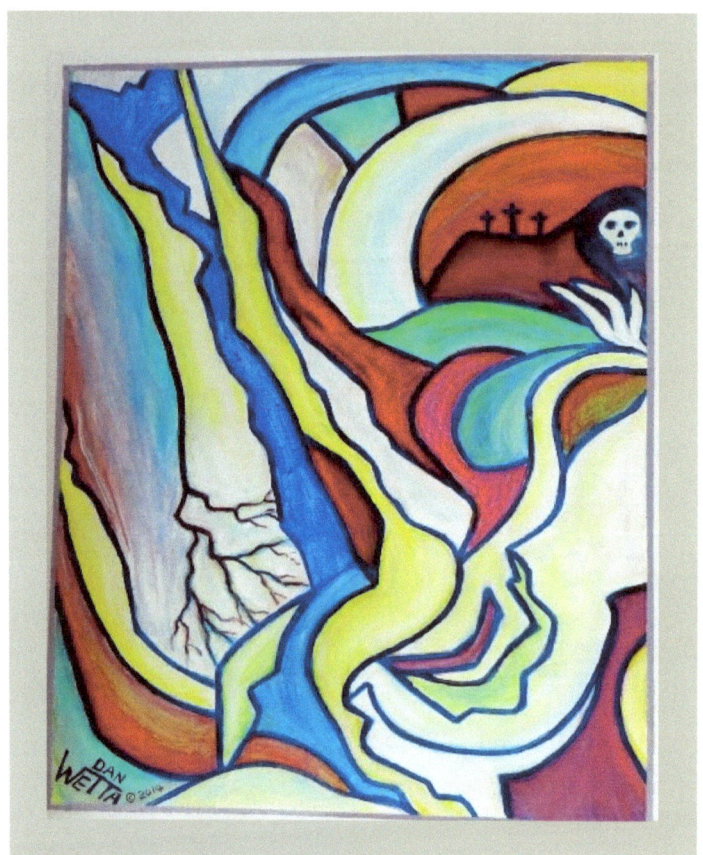

Title: Abstract Mount Golgatha
Size: 30 x 40 inches
Copyright by Dan Wetta 2014

Color stimulates the brain, and abstracts stimulate imagination, but each viewer's imagination will be different.

The title of an abstract affects what the viewer imagines. A person familiar with the bible will think about the crucifixion of Jesus, whereas if I had not given a title to the abstract, a viewer familiar with history might be inclined to reflect upon the horror of ancient Roman punishment.

Chapter 15: A Run-of-the-Mill Dream

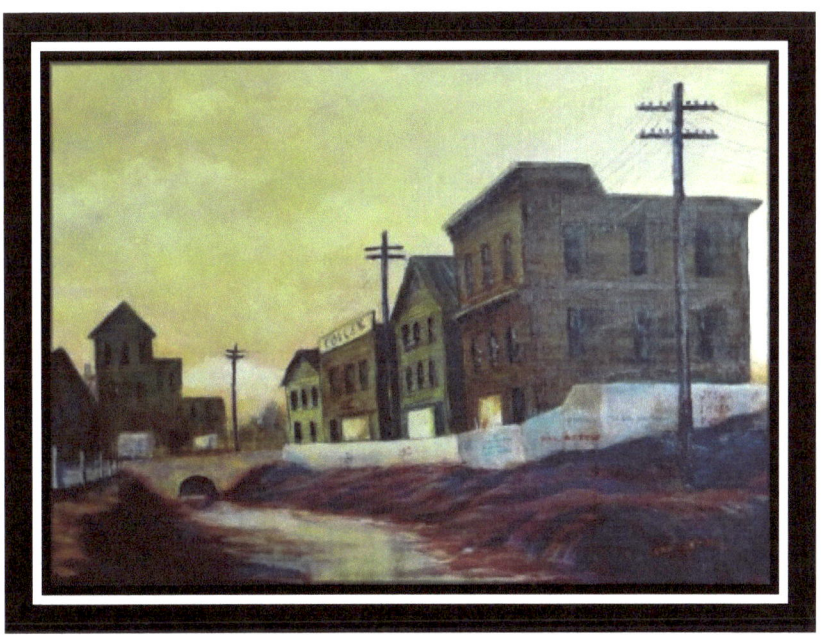

Title: Old Mill Town
Size: 18x23 inches
Medium: Oil on canvas board
Copyright by Dan Wetta 1968

This is one of the oil paintings that I used to do in the 1960's. I switched to acrylics around 1970.

I was driving from Virginia to New Orleans in 1967, when I got lost in this town and began driving around in circles, like you do when lost in the woods. After about fifteen minutes, I said to my wife, "Three months from now, we'll still be driving around in this town." She laughed. Martha had a good sense of humor. I finally got back on the road to New Orleans. There were few interstate highways back then. If you took a long trip by car, you would drive through one small town after another, and, in between towns, you had to watch out for cows on the road.

One time I had been driving for several hours when I came to the top of a hill and slammed on my brakes to avoid hitting a bunch of cows. But there were no cows! I was having a road-weary hallucination. I said to my wife, "I need some sleep! We have to find a place to spend the night."

It might have been then that I had the dream…

RUN OF THE MILL DREAM: SCENE ONE

My dream begins with me walking past a Run of the Mill barber shop, and as you know, you can read minds in a dream. So I knew what that barber was telling his customer, Sam.

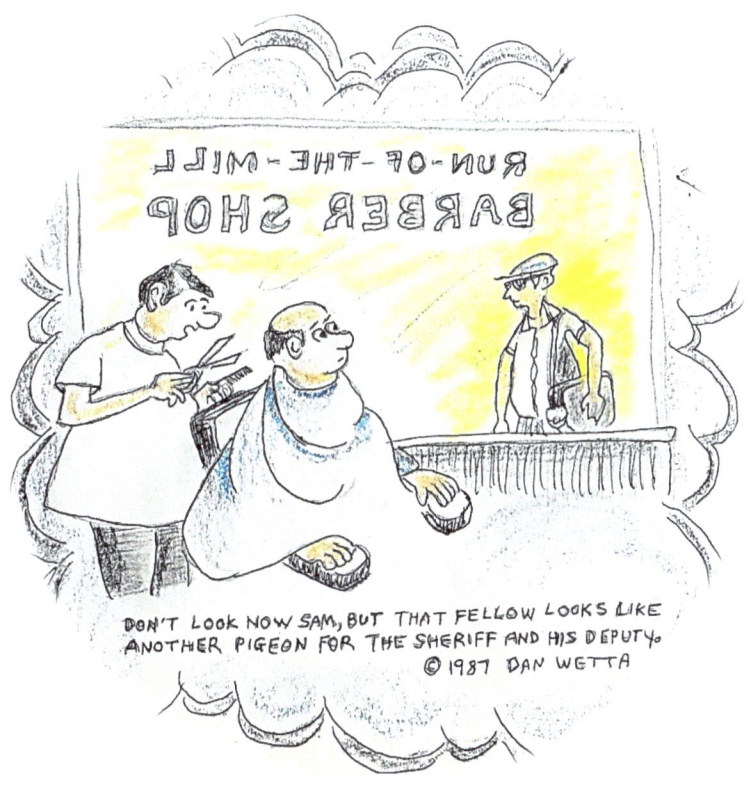

DON'T LOOK NOW SAM, BUT THAT FELLOW LOOKS LIKE ANOTHER PIGEON FOR THE SHERIFF AND HIS DEPUTY.
© 1987 DAN WETTA

Even though the barber's remark would normally have caused me to get out of that Run of the Mill town, I was not thinking normally – in a dream, your brain is not functioning properly.

RUN OF THE MILL DREAM: SCENE TWO

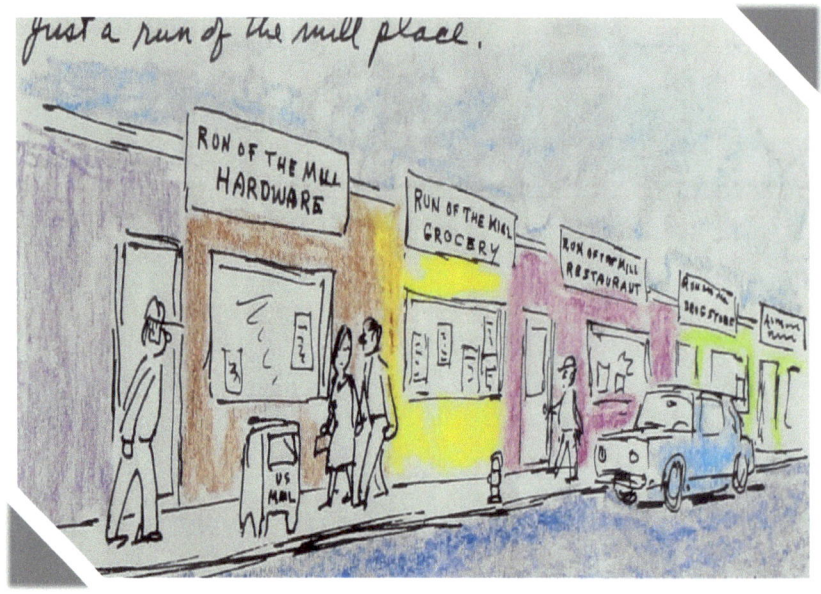

In my dream here, I was feeling hungry, so I went into a Run of the Mill restaurant for something to eat. The sandwich was okay, not especially good, not bad either, just Run of the Mill. Even the customers looked to be Run of the Mill. When I finished the sandwich, I paid the bill, and left a Run of the Mill tip for the waitress.

I began wandering around the Run of the Mill town, and, unfortunately, I strolled into the bad section of town.

My dream continues at Run of the Mill Dream, Scene Three

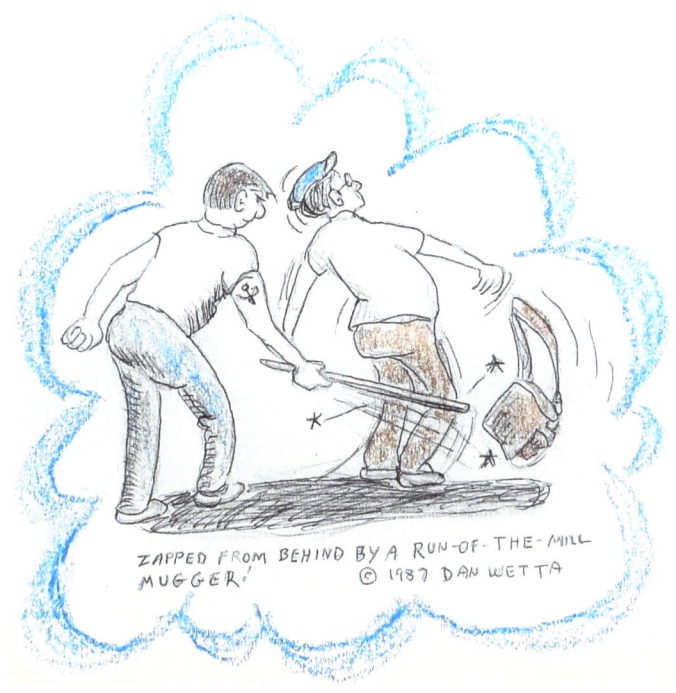

A Run of the Mill mugger zapped me behind the knees with his mugging stick, and I went down. On the way down, my shoulder bag went flying off. The mugger caught it and ran away with it. Since there was no money in the bag, or anything that would be of value to the mugger, only my art supplies, I figured he would discard the bag. Sure enough, I found the bag around the corner, but all my sketching papers and supplies were scattered all over.

RUN OF THE MILL DREAM: SCENE FOUR

While I was trying to gather everything together, a Sheriff went driving by. He slammed on the brakes and backed up. He came over to me and said: "We don't allow no littering in this town, boy." I tried to explain the situation to him, but he ignored it, and said I could pay a twenty five dollar fine or spend five days in his Run of the Mill jail. I paid the fine to the magistrate, and continued looking for something interesting to paint.

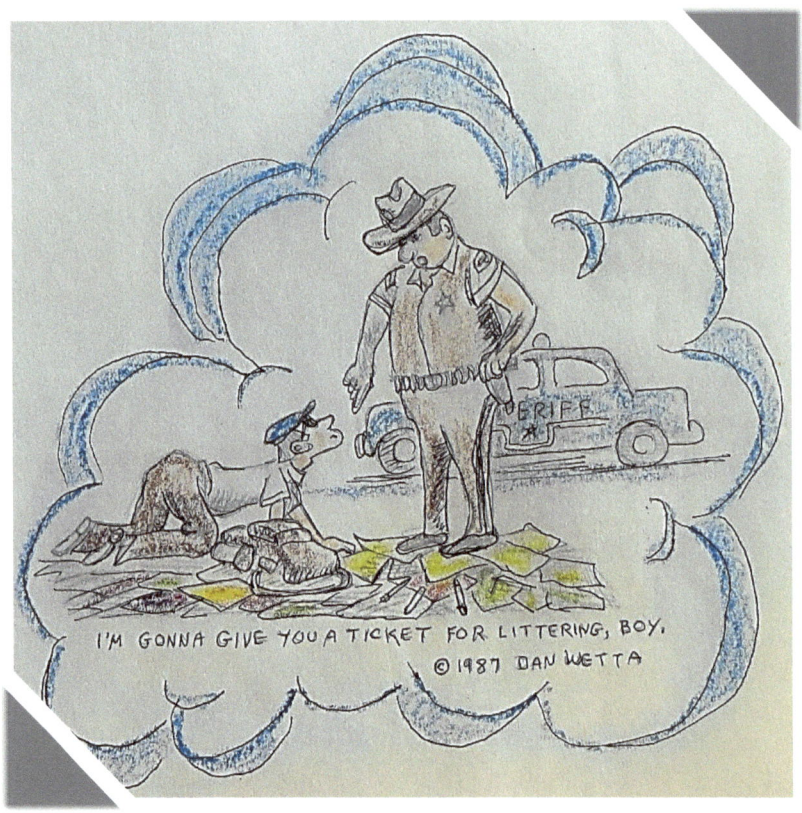

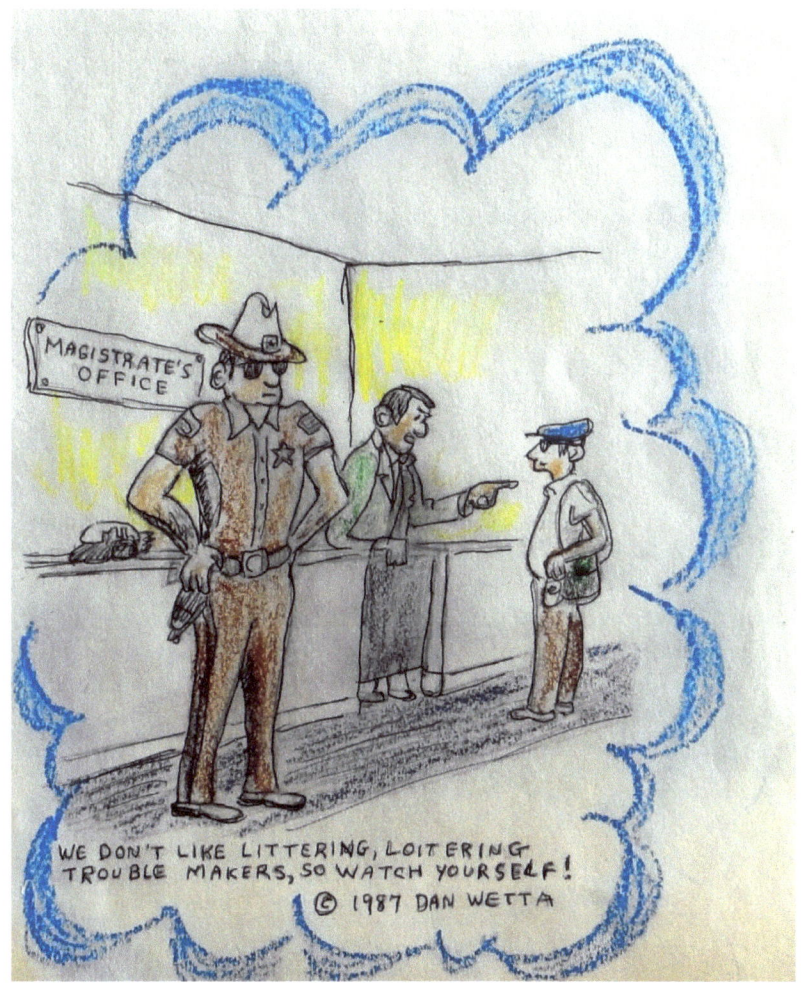

After I paid the fine for littering, I continued to roam around the Run of the Mill town. I was very tired, so I decided to sit down under a tree and rest for a little while. Just about that time, another Sheriff's deputy saw me as he went driving by. He slammed on the brakes and backed up. He walked up to me and wanted to know what I was doing. I said I was just resting. He said I was loitering and that I would have to pay a $75-dollar-fine or go to jail.

I said that I had just paid a fine for littering. He said: "This is for loitering, not littering. Don't you know the difference between littering and loitering, boy?"

RUN OF THE MILL DREAM: SCENE SIX

My dream brain suddenly went into gear and told me that I was not in a Run of the Mill dream. I was in a genuine nightmare!

It was time for me to get out of that Run of the Mill town, so I turned into Super Dog and flew away from there.

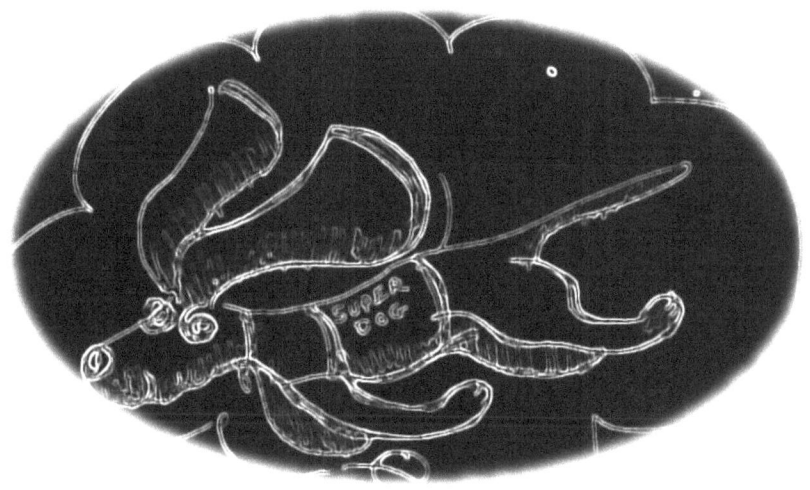

Anybody know how to interpret dreams?

RUN OF THE MILL BOOK ENDING

You probably have done this before, but I thought it would be a nice follow-up to the abstract as a demonstration how your brain is affected by colors:

Stare at the red circle for about 60 seconds.
Then close your eyes gently and you should see a greenish circle with a black hole in the center.
Your brain automatically records the complementary colors.

Title: Stare at this

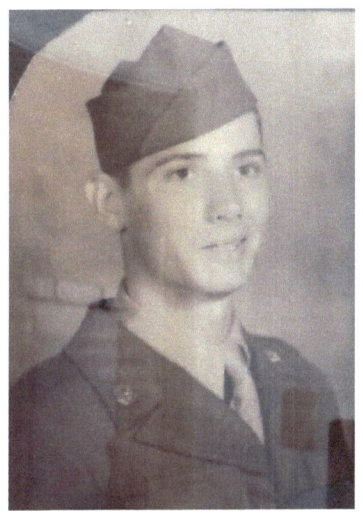

I was born on October 10, 1927, and I grew up during the Great Depression of the 1930's. I enlisted in the army in 1946 and was stationed at Camp Lee, Virginia, near Richmond, where I met my wife and settled down.

My father was a commercial artist, a steel and copper plate engraver for Dameron Pierson Stationery company in New Orleans. He was foreman ot their printing department. One of his tasks was to engrave printing plates to create paper money for Central and South American countries.

I began drawing and painting as a child, but did not want to become a commercial artist like my father because I wanted to paint things that interested me, so I made a living as an accountant-auditor.

I have exhibited at the Virginia Museum of Fine Arts, and was a member of the Richmond Artists' Association for about fifteen years.

We used to have fun exhibiting at malls until one day a City of Richmond Sales Tax Agent came by with a note pad and began writing down the names of artists who did not have a sales tax license.

When I got the city license, the IRS required me to file a quarterly FICA tax form, and the State said I had to have a business license, and then the malls got worried about liability, so they made us buy liability insurance.

Rules and regulations were taking up so much of my painting time that I said, "To heck with it, and I quit exhibiting." As a result, I have acumulated quite a few paintings over the years.

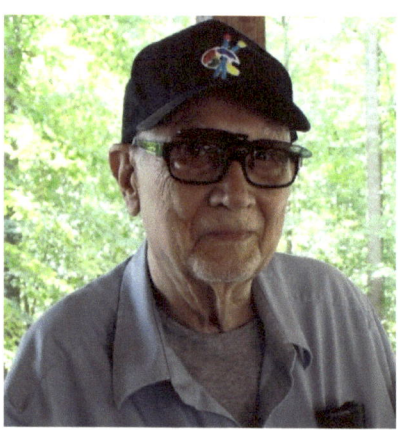